Contents

KU-269-072

Acknowledgements

We are grateful to the following for permission to reproduce copyright material:

Macmillan, London and Basingstoke for extracts from *Nations and Empires: Documents in the Political History of Europe and On Its Relations With the World Since 1648* by Bridges, Dukes, Hargreaves and Scott; Oxford University Press for an extract from a Nineteenth Century German publication, translated by G. A. Kertesz pp. 125–6 of *Documents in the Political History of the European Continent 1815–1939*; George Weidenfeld & Nicolson Ltd. for extracts from *The Rise of the Working Class* by Jurgen Kuczynski.

Seminar Studies in History

Introduction

The Seminar Studies series was conceived by Patrick Richardson, whose experience of teaching history persuaded him of the need for something more substantial than a textbook chapter but less formidable than the specialised full-length academic work. He was also convinced that such studies, although limited in length, should provide an up-to-date and authoritative introduction to the topic under discussion as well as a selection of relevant documents and a comprehensive bibliography.

Patrick Richardson died in 1979, but by that time the Seminar Studies series was firmly established, and it continues to fulfil the role he intended for it. This book, like others in the series, is therefore a living tribute to a gifted and original teacher.

Note on the System of References:
A bold number in round brackets (**5**) in the text refers the reader to the corresponding entry in the Bibliography section at the end of the book. A bold number in square brackets, preceded by 'doc.' [**doc**. **6**] refers the reader to the corresponding item in the section of Documents, which follows the main text. Items followed by an asterisk * are explained in the Glossary.

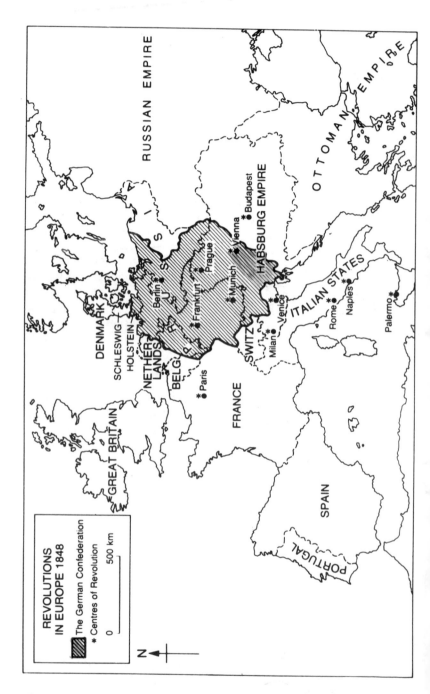

REVOLUTIONS
IN EUROPE 1848

▨ The German Confederation
* Centres of Revolution

0   500 km

N

RUSSIAN EMPIRE

OTTOMAN EMPIRE

HABSBURG EMPIRE

ITALIAN STATES

* Budapest

* Vienna

* Prague

* Munich

* Frankfurt

* Berlin

* Rome
* Naples

* Palermo

● Milan

Venice

SWITZ.

FRANCE

* Paris

SPAIN

PORTUGAL

GREAT BRITAIN

DENMARK

SCHLESWIG

HOLSTEIN

NETHER-
LANDS

BELG.

vi

Part One: The Background

1   The Outbreak of Revolution

On 20 February 1848, the opponents of the French government, which was headed by François Guizot*, made plans to hold a political banquet in Paris. The government banned the banquet and thereby brought the common people of Paris on to the streets of the capital. They marched on the Chamber of Deputies, where their leaders presented a petition demanding Guizot's* resignation.

Popular dissatisfaction with the government, and with Guizot in particular, had been growing during 1847, but the opposition campaign had been led by middle-class politicians who were seeking to reform government rather than overthrow the monarchy of Louis Philippe. Now their cause became, at any rate in appearance, the cause of the common people of Paris, and on 22 February 1848 the police had to clear an unruly crowd in the Place de la Madeleine. The next day the King dismissed Guizot* and called on Louis-Mathieu Molé* to form a government. But the concession had come too late, because on the same evening a great throng of people had made their way along the Boulevard des Capucines to the Ministry of Foreign Affairs, only to find their passage blocked by a troop of cavalry and infantry. According to Victor Hugo, the people at the head of the procession tried to stop and turn aside, 'but the irresistible pressure of the huge crowd weighed on the front ranks'. A shot rang out, and in the panic that followed a whole volley was fired. At least forty people were killed. The victims were piled on a cart lit with torches and within a few hours the city was blocked with barricades (**30**).

On the following morning, 24 February, Alexis de Tocqueville*, a prominent member of the Chamber of Deputies, left his house feeling that he could 'scent revolution in the air'. A group of men gathered round him and asked for news, and he warned them that the only real danger to the government was if they themselves got too excited and took matters to extremes. '"That's all very well, sir," they said, "the government has got itself into this fix by its own fault; so let it get itself out as best it can . . ."' (**7**). Louis Philippe had done just that – he had abdicated that same afternoon

1

and a provisional government had been set up.

The provisional government would probably have decided in favour of a regency, but a series of invasions of the Chamber of Deputies by republican activists, students and eventually a crowd of workers on the afternoon of 24 February pushed the provisional government reluctantly towards the declaration of a republic. Paris was now in the hands of the workers and the 'dangerous classes'. Earlier that day they had invaded the Tuileries Palace and dumped Louis Philippe's empty throne in the courtyard. According to Flaubert the 'common herd ironically wrapped themselves in laces and cashmeres . . . Hats with ostrich feathers adorned blacksmiths' heads, and ribbons of the Legion of Honour supplied waistbands for the prostitutes' (quoted in **30**). Lamartine, who was popular with the people, nevertheless witnessed the invasion of the Chamber of Deputies with fear:

> They crowded the corridors, and rushed with their cries of mortal combat into the spectators' galleries. Their clothes torn, their shirts open, their arms bare, their fists clenched and resembling muscular clubs, their hair wildly dishevelled and singed with cartridges, their countenances maddened with the delirium of revolution, their eyes smitten with the spectacle, so novel to them, presented by this Chamber . . . all revealed them to be desperadoes, who were come to make the last assault on the last refuge of royalty (**74**).

The crowd was armed with pikes, bayonets and sabres. 'Down with the Regency!' they shouted. 'The Republic forever.' The crowd had probably obtained their weapons from units of the National Guard, a volunteer citizens' militia, who had capitulated with little or no resistance. Whatever the precise details of the Guard's activity, it is clear that only one legion, largely recruited from the more prosperous right bank, and half of the Tenth Legion, actively followed orders. Elsewhere there was indifference, and in some cases the guardsmen actually defended the crowds from the troops (**66**). All this served to paralyse the forces of order, thus allowing the revolutionaries to gain the initiative. Once the crowd had made its way into the Chamber, it was then able to force the government to include socialist members, among them Louis Blanc*, as well as a solitary but symbolic worker, Alexandre Albert.

The revolution in France was followed by outbreaks of violence and revolutionary activity elsewhere in Europe. In southern Germany the peasants of the Odenwald and Schwarzwald descended on their landlords' castles and destroyed the charters that perpetuated their feudal obligations. In Bavaria the revolution was intertwined with an old-style Court scandal. King Ludwig's infatuation with a dark-eyed beauty, Lola Montez, had led him to consult her on political matters. He made her Countess of Landsberg, despite protests from ministers, the clergy and even the Pope. Her arrogance and insulting behaviour so incensed the students at the University of Munich that they launched an attack on her house in February 1848. The King attempted to have the university closed, but the news of the abdication of Louis Philippe brought crowds onto the street calling for a republic. Ludwig was forced to banish his beloved Lola and he soon abdicated, leaving the throne to his son, Maximilian. But it was not just the opposition in the streets that had forced Ludwig's hand: it was also the dissatisfaction among the business and professional classes who were demanding a more liberal regime.

By March the revolutionary tide had spread eastwards to Berlin, the capital of Prussia, and to Vienna, Prague and Budapest. It was for long assumed that the rest of Europe was merely following the French example – a view embodied in the writings of the historian Jules Michelet, whose assumptions about the primacy of French culture led to the conclusion that anything which happened in France was 'an event of European significance' (**22**). The fact is that events in Europe had been assuming menacing proportions before the outbreak of revolution in Paris. In 1846 and 1847 the potato crop had been destroyed by disease, causing food riots among the poorer classes of central Europe (**51**, **59**). Meanwhile, a financial crisis affecting the investing classes, as well as causing unemployment, had stoked up resentments among a wide range of social groups. There had been riots in Milan in January 1848 and these culminated in the famous 'five days'' street fighting in March, when the Milanese succeeded in expelling the Austrian garrison. January had also seen an insurrection in Palermo in Sicily. But economic discontent alone is insufficient to explain the widespread nature of the revolutions, for had it been, then they would probably have occurred in 1847, which was the low-point in both the agricultural and financial crises.

The revolutions of 1848 had two important features. First, they were widespread – there were even revolutions in Pernambuco in South America and later in Colombia. Secondly, they were initially successful. In Prussia King Frederick William IV temporarily went with the revolution, parading the streets swathed in the German national flag. But the most startling victory of the revolutionary year was the resignation of Metternich, not only the principal architect of the settlement of 1815, but for many the symbol of order and stability in Europe. Troubles in Vienna had grown from the moment that the news of the revolution in Paris arrived. On 13 March the Diet of Lower Austria, a traditional assembly that contained some liberal-minded nobles, was invaded by a crowd of workers and students (**152, 159**). Metternich argued, along with Windischgratz, the Provincial Governor of Bohemia, that swift action would quell the uprising. But it was too late. Metternich had lost the support of the Court and was soon to lose the ability to take the decisive action that he claimed was necessary. So it was against a background of popular revolution in the streets that Metternich resigned and eventually made his way to England as an exile.

The great Habsburg Empire, which Metternich had so long maintained, seemed on the point of disintegration. The Italians of Lombardy and Venetia were seeking to break free from the grip of Vienna; the Hungarians led by Kossuth were staking their claim for independence; and the first rumblings of Czech nationalism were making themselves heard in Prague. This vigorous activity was not caused solely by the example of the French, even though Michelet's claim of 1846 may seem prophetic: 'France possesses the divine genius of society . . . she is the pilot of the ship of humanity' (quoted in **17**). The outbreak of the revolution in those places already mentioned, as well as in Venice, Rome, Naples, Frankfurt and many of the smaller German states, together with troubles in Ireland and Britain, had general causes to be found in the years before 1848. Of course there were particular causes in different countries but there were nevertheless general European explanations which arose out of the dynamic processes of change that were affecting the whole of European society. It will be necessary to examine these processes and underlying causes in turn.

Part Two: The European Transformation

Beginning in the eighteenth century, Europe had experienced a major transformation. There were two main elements in this. First, there was the onset of industrialisation together with urbanisation, initially in Britain, later in Belgium, and later still in France and Germany. Second, there was the growth of population in the countryside, which not only supplied a ready-made army of migrants for the towns but also placed great strain on the resources of the poorest sections of the rural population. These two major social and economic developments set into motion the long-term strains that contributed so much to the causes of the 1848 revolutions. Of course, the revolutions were also the outcome of political forces that had been released by the great French Revolution of 1789 which had signalled the end of the *ancien régime*. Nevertheless, it is a useful starting point to consider how the major social and economic transformations affected three major social groupings – the working classes, the middle classes and the rural poor. There are two main questions to be answered. Firstly, how did the European transformation affect the fortunes and wellbeing of these three groups? Secondly, did their changing experience in the years before 1848 induce revolutionary attitudes and behaviour?

2 The Impact of Industrialisation on the Working Classes

European writers in the 1830s and 1840s were impressed primarily by the growth of industrial power within their society. The problems of the countryside probably seemed less immediate to them. Nonetheless, the strains of population pressure that were being felt in the countryside should not be ignored by the historian, as it is often less obvious factors that are the springs of great events like revolutions. Contemporary writings, however, show that it was with the pathological problems of urban living – disease,· mortality and overcrowding – that educated society was most concerned. In England, these writings formed part of a debate on the 'Condition of England' question. Similar debates were being carried on among the respectable classes of many European cities. The great fear of the respectable classes was of the urban poor who had already demonstrated their dangerous potential in Paris in 1789 and who continued to show signs of drunkenness, criminality and begging (**64**). The preoccupations of contemporaries are understandable, and the graphic portrayal of working-class misery in many industrial cities – Manchester, Lille, St Etienne – has frequently led historians to begin their accounts of the growth of working-class protest by accumulating evidence of the horrors of urban-industrial living. There is no doubt that the rapid growth of European cities in this period led to a crisis in the areas of municipal services, health and mortality, together with the growth of insanity, suicide, beggary, alcoholism, crime, infanticide and prostitution among the working classes. This has prompted the conclusion that social breakdown, labour protest and even revolution are of the same order (**41**, **64**). However, such a conclusion is based on rather doubtful reasoning, not least because it devalues the coherence of working-class protest activity and fails to appreciate that there is a qualitative difference between behaviour that exhibits a lack of focus and purpose, and actions of protest, which are usually stimulated by specific grievances (**21**).

Before examining the effects of industrial urbanism on the working classes, some account of the extent of industrialisation is necessary. The first general observation to be made is that the continent of Europe was still overwhelmingly rural in 1848. Britain was the most advanced industrial nation and also the most urbanised, yet it was not subject to revolution in 1848. The second most industrialised nation was Belgium, which also managed to avoid revolution. There were probably special reasons for this avoidance (see below, pp. 18–19). However, the absence of revolution in these two advanced industrial states, where working-class misery and privation were extensive, serves as a warning against that line of reasoning which attempts to show a direct relationship between the growth of industry and working-class pauperisation followed by protest and ultimately revolution.

The rest of Europe was fully a generation behind Britain and Belgium in the development of industry (**14**). In France the most significant industrial region was in the north-east of the country based on the textile towns of Lille, Roubaix and Tourcoing. Roger Price has observed that poor transportation facilities, in particular, retarded French economic development (**80**). In technological terms too, France displayed backwardness – for example in the 1840s only forty-one blast furnaces out of a total of 462 used coke, whilst the remainder used charcoal. Poor transportation and abundant supplies of timber from the French forests for charcoal production encouraged manufacturers to stick to older techniques (**93**). The building of railways had also been slow, probably due to a lack of capital. It was this inadequate transport system that prompted the state to enter into the matter of raising finance during Guizot's* administration in the 1840s. All this points to the underdevelopment of industry.

Even though the extent of industrialisation in France was limited compared with England and Belgium, it should not be forgotten that there were some 400,000 factory workers in France by 1848. The growth of factory production disrupted traditional artisanal modes of production. Artisan guilds were under attack from merchants and industrialists; immigrant labour constantly undersold itself in the new factories. Many of the newcomers to the towns were uneducated, and in Mulhouse in the 1840s it has been estimated that three-quarters of the illiterates were born outside the city. These new factory workers were often rootless, showing their discontent by resorting to drink, by abandoning religious practice and by stealing, especially from their place of work (**41, 82, 108**). Such behaviour may indicate a breakdown of the traditional social controls that had prevailed in rural society, and some historians have equated a rise in criminality and social disaffection with an increase in revolutionary protest activity (**108**).

There is no doubt that the condition of the industrial worker was grim. He could expect to die sooner than an agricultural worker, although in Lille the expectation of life of an industrial worker rose from twenty-eight years to thirty-two in the period 1830 to 1848. His diet was extremely monotonous and even the better-paid 'spent at least half their income on starches alone' (**41**). The evidence on working-class living standards and industrialisation is not conclusive – for example, the total meat consumption *per capita* appears to have remained unchanged between 1812 and 1840 (**24**) – but some historians have maintained that the real wages of French workers fell steadily between 1817 and 1848. Further, although the standard of living of the French worker was probably slightly better than his German counterpart (he was less dependent on the potato) his life was often wretched: the working day was often fourteen or fifteen hours compared with about thirteen hours in Germany (**27**). The living conditions of the French worker were exceptionally squalid and he was, of course, vulnerable to disease. The cholera epidemic of 1831–32 carried off 18,400 people in Paris alone in a span of six months. This is a long catalogue of misery and woe. However, it does not in itself provide a complete explanation of revolution.

It is certainly true that the revolutions in France and elsewhere came at the end of a long period of strikes and local rebellions, most notably at Lyon from 1834 onwards, in Toulouse in the 1840s, Limoges in 1847, Lodève throughout the 1840s, Elbeuf and Lille in 1847, Prague in 1844, Silesia in 1844, and Leghorn in 1847. But prior to 1848 this strike activity did not spring mainly from factory workers. In France, the modern industrial sector probably only generated 10 per cent of the strike activity in the Orleanist period. For the most part working-class militancy was instigated by artisans who were materially, albeit marginally, better off than proletarian factory workers.

Despite industrialisation, the traditional artisans continued to form a distinct section within the working class in France, Germany and the cities of the Italian peninsula. For example, in Genoa in 1838 artisans made up almost one-fifth of the total population. In the German states in 1848, artisans still significantly outnumbered factory workers: in Prussia there were about 2.8 million artisans as against 571,000 factory workers. The picture was the same in Bavaria where artisans outnumbered factory workers by slightly more than three to one (**133**). Artisans were often independently employed, as in the case of the master craftsmen silk weavers in Lyon; or they could form conspicuous sections of larger work forces, as in the case of the 800 carpenters and caulkers at the Venice arsenal (**172**). The wellbeing and status of artisans were being undermined almost everywhere, and in France and Germany their guild associations were in the process of being outlawed. Nonetheless, they were quick to form new organisations and some of them became attracted to the new ideology of socialism. It was clear that some of the artisans at Lyon in 1834 had become aware of the writings of Babeuf, Blanqui*, Blanc* and Proudhon. During the revolt the silk weavers 'addressed their remarks to a specific class, the workers; and this, in itself, was new' (**40**).

Lyon is the best example of artisan resistance to the inexorable process of modernisation, but other French cities also displayed a growing artisan militancy. In Toulouse, for example, the local artisanate had been traditionally Catholic-royalist and deferential in its social and political behaviour, presumably because it relied, especially in the luxury trades, on local aristocratic patronage. By the 1830s, however, this patronage was breaking down and by 1846–47 the artisans were allying themselves with the professional men and medium-sized businessmen who were being squeezed as a consequence of competition from the Belgian textile industry. By 1838, 51 per cent of the republican activists were workers and 12 per cent of these were independent master craftsmen (**62**). The key issue for the artisans was the maintenance of some kind of differential economic and status supremacy over the rest of the working class, and their 'relative, if threatened, affluence and a sense of community and professional pride made them the vanguard of worker resistance movements' (**75**). It is hardly surprising that artisans participated in the June Days uprising of 1848 in Paris.

In the German states there was considerable regional variation in the extent of industrialisation. The number of industrial enterprises in Germany before 1848 was small, and even a future giant like Krupp only employed 150 workers in 1846. Industry existed in small isolated pockets – textiles were established in Saxony and coal and iron mining were well developed in Aachen, the Saar and the Ruhr. But as in France there was considerable backwardness: in 1849 only thirty-two out of a total of 247 blast furnaces used coke. Railway development was also retarded. A line had been opened between Nuremburg and Furth in 1835, and in 1837 work had begun on a line between Leipzig and Dresden: but there were still only 549 kilometres of line in 1840. Nevertheless, with the consolidation of the *Zollverein*, a customs union of German states, in 1834 there was considerable potential for industrial development. By 1848 there were almost 600,000 industrial workers in the German states, and Berlin increased its overall population by 100,000 in the 1840s. The German case in particular shows that it was not the extent of industrialisation but rather its nature that depressed the living conditions of the worker. The change from feudalism to capitalism in Prussia was especially rapid. After the Prussian defeat by Napoleon at Jena in 1807, the Prussian state began vigorously to overhaul and reform many aspects of its society. This reform programme included the abolition of hereditary serfdom, which helped to facilitate industrial change. The move toward free-enterprise economics also entailed dismantling the guild associations of German artisans, the *Handwerker*. *Handwerker* protests were becoming increasingly frequent, with outbreaks of unrest in the Palatinate in 1832, Prussia in 1845, Hanover in 1847 and most spectacularly among the Silesian weavers in 1844. Just as in France, it was the squeezing of a traditional social group that resulted in protest and the formulation of a set of demands in the name of the working classes, the 'Industrial Code'*.

There is no doubt that the development of industry in Germany was especially painful for the worker. His standard of living declined, particularly in the 1840s – *per capita* meat consumption fell from 87.6 lb (39.7 kg) in 1844 to 77 lb (34.9 kg) in 1847 [**docs 3a–b**]. The evidence seems to be much more clear-cut here than in the French case, and Hamerow has estimated that the average real wages of German workers declined by 26 per cent in the period 1800–48. At the same time alcohol consumption seems to have risen (reflected in the growth of a lively temperance agitation). But ultimately it was the qualitative change from feudalism to capitalism that led to the weakening of traditional forms of authority and to the marginalising of the *Handwerker*. Their resistance to the growth of free-enterprise capitalism seems to have been the prime motivating force behind the statements of the organised artisans in Germany in 1848 which generally favoured a revival of the guilds, protective duties and guarantees of employment (**133**).

The formulation of a set of demands specifically in the working-class interest leads into a particularly controversial area of historical debate – the question of a special 'class consciousness'. This is a very complex subject and a full analysis would be inappropriate here. It is nevertheless important to indicate at least some of the ideas involved. 'Class consciousness' is a term of special relevance to Marxist historians, because for Marx historical change grew out of conflicts between classes or economic interests. Marx saw the economic organisation of society to be crucially important because changes in the mode of production, for example, led to broader changes in the social organisation. A new language became necessary to describe society. Before industrialisation social commentators spoke of 'ranks', 'degrees' or 'interests' when describing social difference. The term 'working class' first appeared in English writing shortly after 1815; in France the term did not come into popular usage until after 1830. Marx argued that as industrialisation progressed, so each class developed its own consciousness. For the middle classes, or *bourgeoisie*, as Marx called them, the fact that they controlled or owned the forces of production meant that they developed a special belief in freedom of opinion and liberalism generally, as well as a more specific belief in freedom of enterprise. Working-class consciousness, according to Marx, came through the realisation that the middle class owned the means of production. It was this realisation, coupled with a belief that the capitalist middle class was not really essential to the productive process, that would lead the working class to the belief in the necessity of revolutionary socialism. This was the special 'working-class consciousness'. Thus the working-class 'consciousness' was distinct from the middle-class 'consciousness', which favoured reform rather than revolution.

The question of class consciousness is very important to the study of the 1848 revolutions. Did those who took to the streets and lost their lives have a 'consciousness' of their place within society? The question is probably unanswerable in any obvious or categorical sense. It is, however, necessary for the historian to consider whether the transformation of Europe from one type of economic system to another – from feudalism to capitalism – produced a belief among working people in the necessity of revolution as the sole solution to their grievances. For some historians it is almost a matter of faith that the 1848 revolutions were made by the working class, since it was the workers who died on the barricades and fought in the streets. 'It was their hunger that powered the demonstrations that turned into revolutions' (**23**).

How then, did working-class consciousness, in this special Marxist sense, develop? What were the conditions most favourable to its growth? In England, it has been argued that a working-class consciousness emerged out of the struggle for the Reform Bill between 1830 and 1832 (**46**). This view has been refined to take into account local variations. In Oldham, for instance, the presence of a resident capitalist class or *bourgeoisie*, which financed local industry, intensified the sense of working-class consciousness (**20**). That is because the working class could clearly identify the class which was 'exploiting' them in Marx's definition of the word. This class consciousness resulted in the erosion of the separate sectional interests of skilled and unskilled workers – a process which has been measured in Oldham by the level of intermarriage between these two sectional interests. Thus there was a collective interest that cut across the separate interests of skill and status. In other towns in

11

England, such as Northampton, where the shoe industry was financed from London, the absence of a resident capitalist class meant that the development of working-class consciousness was weak or retarded (**20**).

This same pattern may apply to the Continent. For example, following worker riots in Prague in 1844 the Prussian ambassador in Vienna wrote that the disturbances were being inspired by communist beliefs among the workers (**151**). There were apparently indications of solidarity among the workers of Lodève (**33**) that were comparable to those of the workers in Oldham. The growing political awareness of workers in Toulouse was also a consequence of changing structural patterns in the organisation of production (**62**). Elsewhere, in northern Italy for example, the fact that industry was financed from Switzerland and Germany (**14**) may have retarded the development of 'class consciousness' among Italian workers. The only specific working-class demand to emerge in the Venice revolution was the abolition of the salt tax. In France and Germany the working class exhibited a much stronger sense of identity or 'consciousness' by formulating programmes that were intended to ameliorate their condition as workers. It may be, then, that the 1848 revolutions were caused in part by the effect of industrialisation on the working class, in that the latter acquired a more precise awareness of their place within a society that was moving in the direction of industrial capitalism.

The repression of working-class organisations in the post-revolutionary June Days in France and the October Days in Vienna clearly showed the division of interests between the propertied and non-propertied classes. The year 1848 drew the lines of definition. The working-class insurrections failed; the middle-class revolutions had qualified success. After the revolutions the middle classes were able to accelerate the process of industrial expansion, especially in the authoritarian Second Empire and behind the safe confines of the *Zollverein* in Germany. Industrialisation therefore disrupted the traditional world of the artisan in major cities. At the same time, the rural labourers who were forced off the land for one reason or another were unable to reconcile themselves to their new environment (**108**). Consequently any major disaster, such as a food shortage, was likely to produce a violent response.

There is, however, a counterpoint to this argument that the political consciousness of the working class was transformed and that it was formative in the revolutionary outbreak. Factory workers were still relatively few in number, and in nearly all parts of Europe they were outnumbered by artisans. Where they did exist, factory workers were often located in towns that were remote from the centres of political power, and prior to 1848 the strike activity of factory-based workers was lower than that of artisans (**108**). Thus the claim that 'we could virtually omit factory workers from a discussion of the revolutions of 1848 without major distortion' (**42**) might not be disputed even by historians of the left (**32**, **40**). Undoubtedly, the artisans were the key group within the working class: their way of life was under attack and they kicked against the commercial and capitalist cycles that were beginning to dictate their existence.

How far the very poor, the casual labourers, rootless migrants, those who lived on their wits or by criminality, were prominent protagonists in 1848 is extremely difficult to tell. The association between social breakdown and revolution has been well documented (**64**) but the spectre of the 'dangerous classes' was as much a product of middle-class hysteria as anything else (**75**). Studies of Lyon and Marseille (**89**, **107**) show a significant mismatch between political activity, in which artisans were often involved, and criminal activity, in which unskilled labourers were usually the most prominent. However, the claim that the very poor 'lacked the ability to formulate collective goals' (**42**) would seem to be a condescension. In short it is difficult, if not impossible, to generalise about the nature of working-class participation in the 1848 revolutions. All that can be said with certainty is that the revolutions had a powerful politicising effect upon the working classes.

3 The Impact of Industrialisation on the Middle Classes

For some historians the rise of the middle class – in terms of economic and political power – is the outstanding consequence of the process of industrialisation and urbanisation in nineteenth-century Europe (**35**). The middle class is seen as dynamic, leading the way in the process of industrialisation and commercialisation which eventually eroded aristocratic privilege and the monopoly of power enjoyed by the landed classes. Significantly, the 1848 revolutions are seen as a landmark in this process. Admittedly this is questionable, since the resilience of the landed classes and their persistence in controlling crucial aspects of the state apparatus in central and eastern Europe continued until late into the nineteenth century. Nevertheless, it is appropriate here to examine the middle classes in the decades immediately before 1848 to establish whether their experience of change pushed them into the revolutionary camp, or at least into the party of reform.

The middle class in the first half of the nineteenth century was a very broad, amorphous group which is almost impossible to describe without gross generalisation. But for the purpose of simplicity it is convenient to assume that in western Europe it was divided into three broad groups. Firstly, there was the upper middle class of bankers and merchants, together with the most senior state officials as well as the most wealthy industrialists – railway magnates, mine owners and ship owners. In France this group was known collectively as the *grande bourgeoisie*. Some of its members were certainly as wealthy as the great landowners, and the wealthiest members of this *grande bourgeoisie* were part of a social-political elite that also included the nobility. Next in status to this *grande bourgeoisie* were the professional men: lawyers, physicians and surgeons, architects, university professors, journalists and a growing army of bureaucrats and minor state officials. In provincial towns these men often found themselves in the same social *milieu* as the manufacturers. Finally, after the *grande bourgeoisie* and professional men came the lower middle class or *petite bourgeoisie*, sometimes known as the *bourgeoisie populaire*. The *petite bourgeoisie* was a very broad group that included shopkeepers and small traders, elementary-school teachers and small employers. In terms of income and wealth this group was almost indistinguishable from the independent artisans who came immediately below it in the social hierarchy.

The *bourgeoisie* was primarily to be found in the towns and cities as well as some of the larger villages. Its wealth and internal structure varied from place to place. The outlook of the Parisian *bourgeoisie* was markedly different from that of its provincial counterpart. Thus any generalisation about the aspirations and ambitions of this class should be treated with caution. The difficulty of making assertions about the bourgeois groups is well illustrated by the observation of Theodore Zeldin, who has suggested that what distinguished the bourgeois from his contemporaries was his style of life, the way he spent his money, the appearances he endeavoured to maintain, the manners and graces he cultivated (**83**). This kind of social-cultural analysis serves as a reminder that the key issue for the middle classes in the 1840s was not need and want, but rather frustrated ambition. Many sections of that class, especially the professional men and the educated, felt embittered by the lack of recognition they received from society. This will become clearer when each of the three main groups is considered in turn.

In France the *grande bourgeoisie* of manufacturers, merchants and financiers was reckoned to wield considerable, power during the reign of Louis Philippe, a belief reflected in the regime's nickname – the Bourgeois Monarchy. The July Revolution of 1830 has been regarded as a major breakthrough for the *grande bourgeoisie* in political terms. Whereas in 1827, 44 per cent of the deputies in Charles X's Chamber were of noble origin, by 1836 this figure had fallen to 14 per cent. The implication of this fall in noble representation is that bourgeois representation increased. Other public offices experienced a similar pattern, most notably the prefecture, which was also invaded by the *grande bourgeoisie* (**98**). However, revisionist historians have questioned whether the 1830 revolution was so significant in terms of the advent of bourgeois power. For them, 1830 was primarily a triumph for lawyers, bureaucrats and ex-Bonapartist officers, and they claim that the change was essentially one of personnel rather than class (**104, 105**). Moreover, the *bourgeoisie* was such a variegated and divided group that it is difficult to ascribe to it an agreed set of interests, let alone a distinctive ideology or consciousness. Much of this revisionist research is motivated by a desire to refute the original Marxist interpretation of the July Monarchy as a triumph for the financial *bourgeoisie*. But Marx, too, had observed the conflict of interests between the financial railway elite, and the emergent manufacturing *bourgeoisie* which sought cheap credit and lower transport costs. This latter group was beginning to voice its disaffection with the regime by the 1840s. There is no doubt that politically the system was managed by a minority of powerful notables – aristocrats, pseudo-nobles and an *haute bourgeoisie* (**71**). Further, the claim that 1830 was merely a change in personnel disregards the growing interaction between the professional men – particularly lawyers – and businessmen. The business classes had insufficient time to devote to public office and still run their businesses. Lawyers, however, serviced the business classes on a day-to-day basis and were also ideal spokesmen in the political arena. Adolphe Thiers is perhaps the best example. He was a lawyer from the Midi and also a director of the Anzin mining company. He had been prime minister on three occasions between 1830 and 1840 and was a leading opposition figure in the 1840s.

The complex structure of the middle class should not, however, deflect the historian from trying to make some broad generalisations that enable the student to understand the position of the middle class, as well as its role in the 1848 revolutions. In the case of France, the French historian Adeline Daumard attempted a broad quantification and description of the Parisian *bourgeoisie*. She found that in the 1840s 1 per cent of the middle class controlled 30 per cent of all middle-class wealth. This *grande bourgeoisie* was for the most part socially conservative in outlook, often aspiring to the way of life of the aristocracy. It has been observed in this respect that the *bourgeoisie* of Paris preferred to invest in land rather than develop their industrial enterprises, In 1820, 36.5 per cent of those who could vote in parliamentary elections were described as *professions économiques* (businessmen) whereas 46.2 per cent were described as *propriétaires* (property owners). By 1842, however, twelve years after the establishment of the Bourgeois Monarchy, only 29.4 per cent of the electors were described as businessmen, whereas 49.9 per cent were recorded as property owners.

This kind of evidence has been used to conclude that the *grande bourgeoisie* aspired to the status of aristocrats (**41**), but it should be remembered that much bourgeois property investment was based in towns. Further, Roger Price has questioned this view, contending that the July Monarchy did not always accommodate entrepreneurial requirements. Banking structures, for example, were weakly developed and debt was still socially frowned upon. Thus it may not have been the case that the *grande bourgeoisie* simply transferred their investments from enterprise to land, changing their *mentalité* from entrepreneur to *rentier*, but rather that they had to invest in property in order to provide security for any capital venture that they wished to undertake (**77, 78**). In this sense then, the regime of Louis Philippe may have failed to meet bourgeois expectations. Admittedly the regime did introduce a number of measures that favoured businessmen – for instance, tough anti-union legislation in 1834 and a relaxation of the bankruptcy laws in 1838 – but Marx's contention that the July Monarchy was nothing more than a 'joint stock company for the exploitation of France's national wealth' is deceptively simple. The *grande bourgeoisie* was not a revolutionary class, in France at any rate, and in many ways the Orleanist regime was solicitous of its interests. However, there was a sense in which its complacency was jolted in the period 1845–48 when government plans to facilitate railway building backfired (see below, pp. 47–9), causing a stock exchange collapse. In this case Louis Philippe lost the support of the one narrow social group that his regime had apparently cultivated since 1830. Admittedly the causes of the February Revolution stem from a complex of factors – an agricultural crisis, social unrest in industrial towns, a banking crisis and a tax revenue failure – but there is much to be said for the view that the paralysis of business activity led to a 'pervasive lack of confidence' in the regime (**71**).

In other parts of Europe the *grande bourgeoisie* was beginning to represent a small but conspicuous minority in the major cities. In Berlin in 1848 there were 112 merchants out of a total population of 400,000. The captains of industry were small in number but they were often to the fore when demanding the liberalisation of government. Most notable in this respect were Ludolf Camphausen and Gustav Mevissen in Rhenish Prussia; and David Hansemann in Aachen as well as August Borsig in Berlin. The German equivalent of the French *grande bourgeoisie* had many grievances: the political systems of almost all the German states were immobile and dominated by a hereditary aristocracy. This was particularly so in Prussia where the *Junkers* regarded themselves as a closed caste who had a monopoly of public careers in government, the bureaucracy and the army. The German upper middle class was also dissatisfied with the fragmentation of the German market. Admittedly the development of the *Zollverein* went a good way towards achieving economic integration, but the banking system was still unresponsive to entrepreneurial needs as far as credit was concerned.

In the Italian states, it was in the northern regions – Piedmont, Lombardy and Venetia – that industry was most developed. Milan, the capital of Lombardy, was probably the most prosperous city in the whole of the peninsula. A trade directory of 1838 listed forty-two bankers and seventy-six silk merchants, together with 196 manufacturers of silk and cotton goods (**172**). There was a substantial class of more traditional merchants committed to provisioning and basic commodity dealing – grain, olive oil and wine – but the new entrepreneurs were becoming increasingly vocal. There was a growing audience for the writings on political economy produced by the economic writer Cattaneo, whose articles in Milan's *Universal Annals of Statistics*, produced during the 1830s, specifically addressed this class of market-oriented entrepreneurs. The wealth of Lombardy and Venetia was also recognised by the Habsburgs, who had ruled the two provinces since 1815. In fact, their two Italian possessions were the most heavily-taxed part of the Empire, which was understandably a source of considerable grievance for the Lombard and Venetian *bourgeoisie*. According to Cesare Correnti, writing in 1847, it was the tax revenues from these two Italian provinces that sustained the 'dying credit of the Empire' (quoted in **172**). In 1839, businessmen in Venice founded the Venetian Commercial Society. It was particularly critical of what it regarded as the inequity of the Habsburg tax system and it mounted a vigorous campaign against the Habsburg preference for the port of Trieste (**174**).

In the three cases so far considered – France, the German states and the Italian possessions of the Habsburgs – the upper middle class had cause to be dissatisfied to a greater or lesser extent. This was not the case elsewhere – most notably in Belgium and Britain. In both these small countries industrialisation had progressed at a faster pace than in the rest of Europe. In both, the financial and banking system had developed in a responsive way to the requirements of entrepreneurs. By the end of the eighteenth century, the use of shares was more widespread in England than in any other European country. This meant that more capital was available for enterprising schemes, and it is significant that in Britain railway building was sustained entirely by public share subscription. Elsewhere in Europe governments became embroiled in railway schemes, often underwriting the loans, sometimes with unforeseen political consequences (see below, pp. 47–9). In England, the growth of a provincial banking network helped to make more short-term credit available. All this suited entrepreneurs and the upper sections of the middle class generally. The political system, too, was apparently more open. As a special point of comparison, it is worth noting that the 1832 Reform Act in Britain had the effect of enfranchising one in twenty-five inhabitants, whereas the equivalent electoral law in France of the July Monarchy – the 200-franc direct taxation qualification – only enfranchised one in 170 inhabitants. The British system also seemed to be able to sustain legislation that promoted upper-middle-class interests. The Poor Law Amendment Act of 1834 created the free market conditions for cheap wage labour; the Municipal Corporations Act of 1835 effectively handed over the government of the towns to the upper middle class; and finally Peel's free-trade reforms, culminating in the repeal of the Corn Laws in 1846, served to demonstrate that government was flexible and did not exist for the sole purpose of defending aristocratic privilege.

In Belgium, which had won its independence from the Netherlands in 1830, government policy was highly responsive to the demands of industrialists. The *Société générale de Belgique* had been founded during the period of Dutch rule in 1822, and the revolution of 1830 had committed the bank more definitely to industry. Indeed, its board of governors declared that it favoured 'creating and spreading the spirit of association as a means to prosperity for this country's industry'. The bank also founded subsidiary finance companies that were used to create short-term credit. All this suited Belgium's business classes. In the political sphere, too, the government demonstrated a similar flexibility to that shown in Britain, with a broadening of the franchise in 1847. Now, almost all sections of the middle class, including the *petite bourgeoisie*, were admitted within the political pale. The cases of Britain and Belgium are instructive, because in both countries the economic policies of the state were more oriented to the needs of enterprise than in any other part of Europe. In both cases a substantial element of the middle class now participated in official political life. In both cases there were timely concessions immediately before 1848 – the franchise in Belgium and the repeal of the Corn Laws in Britain – which served to appease middle-class discontent sufficiently to avoid revolution. Yet while there is a good deal of truth in the argument that Britain and Belgium avoided revolution because their respective middle classes were accommodated, whereas France, Germany and the Habsburg territories were plunged into revolution precisely because they failed to meet middle-class demands, this is not the whole truth. There were other factors at work and these will be considered later.

Next in status to the upper middle class of industrialists and financiers were the professional men: lawyers, doctors, and university teachers. In western Europe this group probably represented as much as 10 per cent of the whole of the middle class (**33**). The professional classes developed with the growth of state bureaucracy and the associated increase in the training of state officials (**57**). Such training, in turn, required a general expansion of state education so that aspirants to the professions could be prepared for the entrance examinations. In France, for example, attendance at *lycées* doubled between 1809 and 1842. This educational expansion tended to benefit the sons of the *grande bourgeoisie*, and places at the *École Polytechnique* were dominated by them (**75**). This institution was expected to produce suitable candidates for the elite positions of the civil service, but not all the young men who experienced such an education found their way into the coveted positions of the state bureaucracy. Although many entered the professions of law and medicine, there were still many others whose ambition for a public position went unsatisfied.

Competition for office, a key means of achieving social recognition, was a potent source of dissatisfaction with the regime of Louis Philippe. It made little difference whether or not an office was elective, for wealth exerted its influence at all levels, and educated men of only moderate means found themselves in effect political outsiders. They were under-represented even in the Chamber of Deputies, for here as elsewhere the rich were predominant. In 1840 two-thirds of the 459 deputies in the Chamber paid more than 1000 francs per annum in direct taxation, yet in the country as a whole only 18,000 Frenchmen were taxed at this high level. Many professional men were not sufficiently wealthy even to qualify for the vote in Louis Philippe's reign, although the electorate increased from 160,000 in 1830 to 240,000 by 1846 (**65**). Guizot*, the dominant politician of the July Monarchy, argued that this natural increase would continue as the country became more wealthy (**47**) but in the meantime many educated men were extremely dissatisfied with the regime. A good example of its narrow base is revealed by the case of Victor Cousin, a professor at the Sorbonne, who even became a cabinet minister, but whose earnings were insufficient for him to qualify for the vote under the 200-franc electoral law (**18**).

In central and eastern Europe academics were often the articulate spokesmen for the new political programmes. Palacky, the Czech historian, is perhaps the most notable example, but there were others such as Dahlmann, Rotteck and Welcker in the German universities; Franz Pulsky, the Hungarian journalist active in Vienna, who translated Kossuth's famous Pressburg speech* in 1848; and Montanelle and Pigli at the University of Pisa, in Italy. It was academics, especially in Germany, who provided the liberal movement with most of its ideas. The picture in France was similar, with professors such as Michelet and Quinet acting as the intellectual spokesmen of republicanism. In the German states the educated classes were particularly disaffected, for the competition for state office was especially acute. In Prussia the civil service was dominated by the aristocracy. A legal education was a prerequisite for obtaining a state post and the number of law students in Prussian universities increased by almost a third in the decade after 1841. To compensate for this overproduction of law students, the state introduced a more rigorous entrance examination for the civil service, with the result that a 25 per cent failure rate was achieved. Further, those who passed the examination had to serve an arduous apprenticeship, during which they received no pay. In 1848 there were about 4000 legal apprentices in the system. Between 1836 and 1848 the judicial branch offered about twenty positions a year. The waiting list became so long that about ten candidates a year actually died without ever gaining a post. Those who escaped death were required to maintain an expensive front and their general behaviour was kept under close scrutiny by the police (**41**, **57**) [**doc. 1c**].

This frustration within the educated classes was perhaps most acutely felt within the student ranks; and there were a number of politically motivated student organisations, of which the *Burscenschaften* is the most well known. Students were certainly active in 1848, and in Vienna they formed an Academic Legion. In France, too, students were interested in political matters, but whether students formed the 'nucleus of the demonstrators who started the revolution', as Zeldin claims (**83**), or were merely part of the crowd (**38**), is uncertain. All in all, the anxiety and frustration about future prospects experienced by educated groups throughout Europe were of major importance in the 1848 revolutions since it was these groups that articulated the political programmes in the early stages of the reform movement. The words of an Orleanist official are certainly appropriate here: 'it isn't the workers one should fear, rather it is the *déclassés*, doctors without patients, lawyers without briefs, all of the misunderstood, the discontented, who finding no place at the banquet table try to overturn it. In Paris for every 1200 reading for the law, 20 achieve fame, 80 fortune, 200 a modest living – the rest vegetate' (quoted in **75**).

After the *grande bourgeoisie* and the professional classes, the third group to be considered within the general bracket of the middle class is the *petite bourgeoisie*, composed principally of shopkeepers, small employers and low-grade clerks. As a group, the *petite bourgeoisie* was frequently vulnerable to credit problems. However, these lower-middle-class men often shared the same political aspirations as their more illustrious bourgeois counterparts. Consequently, their economic vulnerability, combined with their political interests, made them an ideal political bridging-point between the upper sections of the *bourgeoisie* and the independent artisans (**38**). In France, the *petite bourgeoisie* were not usually rich enough to qualify for the 200-franc franchise and they became highly critical of Guizot's* rule. Furthermore, they prided themselves on their independence and respectability and were avid readers of the newly growing popular press which highlighted the scandals and corruption of the Guizot period. These revelations helped to turn them away from the Orleanist regime which had so little to offer them, but it was economic factors that really alienated the *petite bourgeoisie* – as Ledru-Rollin recognised when he warned Louis Philippe that 'All the retailers who were your supporters, will rise against you'. Their discontent was still apparent in 1848 itself, for although the June Days uprisings were essentially an artisan and worker affair, and large numbers of shopkeepers were to be found supporting the campaign for order as represented by Cavaignac, there were nonetheless 119 jewellers and 191 wine merchants arrested out of a total of 11,693 (**40**).

Elsewhere in Europe the lower middle class was often to be found in alliance with the artisans. This was particularly the case in the German states where shopkeepers railed against the laws of Jewish emancipation, venting their frustration in the form of proto-anti-Semitic programmes to revoke the licences of Jewish peddlers and hawkers (**133**, **141**).

How then can the position of the middle classes be best summarised? The upper middle class of financiers, elite state officials and manufacturers with major export interests had enjoyed some success in the period 1830–48. This was especially the case in Britain and Belgium and to a lesser extent in France. Elsewhere in central and southern Europe, the business classes had great difficulty in realising their ambitions and bending the state to policies that promoted economic progress. Even in those states where middle-class ambition had been recognised, middle-class confidence was seriously impaired in the period 1845–48. In France, particularly, the *grande bourgeoisie* began to despair of the regime of Louis Philippe, and in Europe as a whole the upper sections of the middle class remained discontented and frustrated. In Germany, the Habsburg Empire and the Italian states they had no 'rights of political participation'

(**42**). The middle class of professional men – intellectuals, journalists, medical men and lawyers – were often the spokesmen of a general middle-class discontent. These middle-class professionals and educated men found great difficulty in achieving what they thought was just political and social recognition. East of the Rhine it was these groups, especially, that were the most politicised. Most of their arguments, however, were reformist, not revolutionary, and most of them were surprised when revolution broke out, which explains their singular lack of ability to keep control of a rapidly changing situation. Finally, the lower middle class harboured resentment and frustration stemming from its growing economic marginality in society. The combined dissatisfactions of all three sections of the middle class were undoubtedly crucial. Each section of the middle class had some cause for dissatisfaction – inadequate banking facilities, lack of social and political recognition, expensive short-term credit – but the middle class as a whole was well placed to articulate its discontent and mobilise it into political pressure.

4 Population Pressure and the Condition of Agricultural Society

The changes that have been outlined so far primarily affected urban life. In order to understand the causes of the 1848 revolutions more fully, it is necessary to appreciate the great pressure that was placed on the agricultural system from the middle of the eighteenth century onwards. Crudely put, this was a matter of numbers. In the middle of the eighteenth century the population of Europe was 120 to 140 million; by 1800 this had risen to 187 million and by 1840 to 266 million. This growth was not entirely due to urban development. In Germany some rural areas showed a more dramatic population growth than some urban areas. For example, in the substantially rural areas of Pomerania, in eastern Prussia, the population swelled from 683,000 in 1816 to 1,198,000 in 1849 – a 75 per cent increase. The population of the industrial region of Arnsberg-Dusseldorf on the other hand grew from 968,000 in 1816 to 1,198,000 in 1849 – only a 24 per cent increase. More significantly, perhaps, for arguing that the causes of the 1848 revolutions were to be found in the deteriorating conditions of rural society, at least as far as timing was concerned, the Pomeranian population increased by 1.41 per cent per annum between 1840 and 1849, whereas the population of Arnsberg-Dusseldorf increased by only 1.18 per cent per annum in the same period (**48**). Such a rate of growth put great pressure on food supplies, and by the 1840s many parts of Europe were over-populated, in the sense that food supply was insufficient and that there was growing underemployment among many sections of the population.

Population pressure naturally caused migration. Many people emigrated beyond Europe, but there were extensive movements within the continent. These exhibited great variety and complexity. Some shifts were of a permanent nature, being rural–urban movements brought about by the complex interplay of push and pull factors. New immigrants to industrial towns were invariably prepared to sell their labour more cheaply than those workers already established there. This caused conflicts in such cities as Lille (**51**), Marseille (**107**), Paris (**64**), Milan (**172**) and Venice (**174**). There

24

were also numerous temporary migrations, often of a circular nature: peasants in the French Limousin frequently migrated on a seasonal basis to work in the building trades in Paris and Lyon (**75**). In upland Aquitaine peasants would migrate to Languedoc to work on the harvest, and the peasant women of Morvan often travelled to become wet nurses for bourgeois families in nearby towns. These temporary migrations indicate the economic pressures that the rural population was experiencing. At the same time these movements brought them into contact with townsmen from whom they may have learnt new ideas (**61**). It should not be assumed that the peasantry were a uniform mass, always on the side of political conservatism and reaction.

Apart from food shortages and seasonal unemployment the rural population of Europe was frequently prey to natural disaster – disease, famine and floods, as well as intermittent fluctuations in food prices [**doc. 4**]. In Upper Silesia, for example, there had been heavy flooding in 1847 followed almost immediately by drought. Hunger and typhus ensued (**139**). Very often the response of the rural poor to such disasters was to seek vengeance on the privileged and the powerful; and the wealthier classes of the countryside often lived in fear of incipient uprising and riot. At the same time, changes in the modes of agricultural production and the extent of capital investment had the effect of squeezing out the small independent peasant producers. This often pushed the rural classes into proto-industrial activities, especially in textiles. Rural industries existed in areas around Aachen (**111**); in the Pays de Caux, especially around Rouen (**75**); and very extensively in Silesia (**139**).

The growing capitalisation of the countryside had specific effects on the peasantry. In France, for example, the Forest Code of 1827 had facilitated the purchase of communal forests by private landowners, and this denied the peasantry ancient and traditional foraging rights. Consequently there were numerous disputes between peasants and forest guards in the Ariège, where there were over 2000 convictions for the breaking of the forest laws in 1844 alone. In 1848 it was in central and southern France that peasant unrest was most acute, and it was in these regions that more traditional modes of agriculture and ancient peasant rights clashed most sharply with the incursion of new private enterprise (**61, 75**). Where a form of capitalist agriculture was already well established, as in northern France, then peasant discontent was minimal. Elsewhere in Europe, the diversity of peasant discontent manifested itself in numerous ways. Peasants around Belluno in Habsburg Venetia had had their personal possessions – kettles and bedsteads – confiscated because they defaulted on their tax payments (**174**). In Teschen, in the Habsburg Empire, peasants attacked the Larisch Palace in September 1847 demanding an end to their labour service under the *Robot** as well as the abolition of punishment by the lash. Throughout the 1840s, then, those who had been pushed to the margins of existence in the countryside were drawn to acts of violence which were designed to exact retribution or achieve some form of elementary justice. Attacks on money-lenders and usurers were rife in Alpine France as well as in southern Germany (**59**).

There were also changes that affected the class relations of those who lived on the land. At the beginning of the nineteenth century, aristocrats still held important political positions in most European states. In Britain the aristocratic control over government was such that between 1832 and 1866 only twelve ministers in the cabinet were lawyers and five were businessmen, whereas sixty-four were from aristocratic families. Elsewhere in Europe the aristocracy formed the core of the political class and dominated positions in the state bureaucracy, the Church and the army. Only in France, where the Revolution of 1789 had adulterated the pure *noblesse*, could it be said that the traditional aristocracy had been decisively excluded from power. In central and eastern Europe the nobility still exercised considerable power through provincial assemblies, where they had control over taxation and administration. In Prussia nine out of eleven ministers, twenty-nine out of thirty diplomats, twenty out of twenty-eight provincial governors and 7,264 out of 9,434 army officers were *Junkers* (**42**). Aristocratic honour in Prussia was also given legal recognition: an aristocrat's word in a court of law was accepted without an affidavit. Of course such privileges were closely guarded by the aristocracy, and it was their actions and fears that determined the nature of political rule between 1815 and 1848; in the long run, therefore, these actions were important causes of the 1848 revolutions.

The political power of the aristocracy was derived from land. Land was the great measure of wealth. In Britain 500 members of the peerage owned half the total acreage at the beginning of the nineteenth century. In Prussia, east of the Elbe, it was the *Junkers* who dominated; in Silesia alone half the total acreage was owned by fifty-four families. In the Habsburg lands the concentration of landownership was unparalleled except in Russia, and in the province of Hungary the number of truly large landowners or 'magnates' did not exceed 200 families (**30**).

This highly concentrated patter.. of landownership did not apply in France, where half the land was owned by 2.7 million peasant proprietors. There were still a number of noble and bourgeois owners, who possessed some 20 per cent of the land which they in turn leased to peasant tenant farmers. Within the peasant class there was also great diversity. Some peasants, especially in the Alpine regions, were little more than subsistence farmers; whilst others, in the wine-growing regions, were virtually mini-capitalists. But many of these independent producers lacked credit and often carried a heavy burden of taxation (**109**). There were still some very large estates in western France of between 200 and 400 hectares, and the owners of these lands still retained their status as provincial notables with all the power and privilege that their titles implied.

In addition to owning large tracts of land, the European aristocracy also controlled the lives of vast sections of humanity, principally those peasants who were still subject to some form of feudal due. The condition of the peasantry, especially in central and eastern Europe, was one of the most important factors affecting the stability of society. The peasantry had often proved volatile, and their participation in the French Revolution of 1789 was well recognised by owners of property. In central and eastern Europe there were numerous examples of peasant disorder (**138**, **139**) but the peasant uprising against the Polish nobility was perhaps the most spectacular. Metternich's appeal to the peasantry to rise against the Polish nobles' national rebellion was a two-edged sword. The viciousness with which the Polish peasants attacked their Polish masters was viewed with trepidation by all landowners, irrespective of their nationality.

The latent violence of the peasantry may well be explained by the wretchedness of their condition. Some 70 per cent of their income was spent on food (**41**). Therefore, any rapid increase in the price of bread or potatoes was bound to bring the most extreme hardship. Grievances over feudal payments were ongoing and in the Habsburg territories it has been observed that the full-scale revolution of 1848 in effect 'forestalled a separate peasant revolution' (**148**). The deep-rooted nature of the tensions that existed in European rural society defies exhaustive treatment here. However, it should not be thought that the food crisis of 1845–47 was some short-term disaster, some accident, that helps to explain the timing of the 1848 revolutions. The possibility of harvest failure was inherent in the European system of agriculture, and the poor nature of transport intensified the problem. Moreover, growing population and intense pressure to

27

raise the efficiency of production pushed the poorest and least-equipped sections of the population to the margins of existence. At the same time, the hierarchical system of deference and dependency was breaking down, so that when the food crisis struck in 1845–47 the fragile stability of rural society disintegrated. Thus although the political programmes were articulated in the towns there was an underlying vulnerability, not only in the countryside's productive mechanisms but also in its social stability. This startled contemporaries, both rural and urban, and certainly contributed to the collective *malaise* that gripped the ruling elites in 1847 and 1848.

5   The Breakdown of Traditional Political Control

Just as the forces of economic and social change disrupted the traditional world of almost all classes, particularly the artisans in the cities and the peasants in the countryside, so they also affected the official institutions of the state. Until the French Revolution of 1789 the rule of kings had not been seriously questioned on the continent of Europe. The turmoil that followed in the wake of the execution of Louis XVI in France determined the statesmen at Vienna in 1815 to restore the power of monarchy and, with it, general political stability. The Vienna Settlement was more, then, than just a set of territorial arrangements between the major powers of Europe; it was also a general political settlement that aimed to bring about the reassertion of the ideas of the *ancien régime* – legitimate monarchy, the authority of the Church and the privilege of the aristocracy [**doc. 1a**].

In the decade after 1815 European statesmen strove to maintain the principles of the *ancien régime* against the insidious threat of radical jacobinism, nationalism and even limited constitutional government. Metternich's Carlsbad Decrees of September 1819 [**doc. 1c**] had their equivalent in the repressive Six Acts passed in Britain in the same year. Metternich had good cause to be concerned, as the years immediately after 1815 were punctuated by a number of revolutionary outbreaks in Spain, Naples and Greece. The political reaction that followed these outbreaks was generally severe – in Naples the King appointed a Minister of Vengeance to wage a counter-revolution (**171**); in Lombardy and Venetia the garrisons were strengthened and political conspirators were imprisoned (**148**). The spectre of revolution was always at the forefront of the minds of the kings and ruling statesmen of Europe from 1815 to 1848; and it was this fear of revolution that often determined the decisions they took.

The danger of revolution was highly developed in the mind of Metternich, although the actual possibility of revolution was probably most real in France. The statesmen at Vienna had worked to provide stability in France by restoring the Bourbon monarchy in the person of Louis XVIII. However, it was recognised that unmitigated reaction was not feasible, and that some form of compromise was needed. Napoleon's Senate had tried to salvage some of the benefits of the Revolution when, in 1814, it drew up a constitutional charter which sought to establish the inviolability of liberal principles – which were, in fact, later accepted by Louis XVIII. But Louis' exile in England during the Revolutionary and Napoleonic years 'had not taught him the virtues of parliamentary government' (**65**). Nonetheless he appeared to accept a voluntary curtailment of his prerogative, and he agreed to the establishment of a representative element in the constitution in the form of a Chamber of Deputies. The King, however, retained considerable powers, being the sole initiator of legislation, with the Chamber being expected to vote only on the submissions made to it by ministers whom the King had chosen. Further, article 14 of the constitution deposited the issue of state security firmly in the hands of the King. Although the constitution appeared to be a compromise between royal prerogative and bourgeois interests, the power of the monarchy in France was considerable after 1815, even if the French monarchy was less autocratic than its other Continental counterparts. It was still predisposed towards the old habits of patronage, favouritism and Court intrigue. Louis XVIII's infatuation for Mme du Cayla led to the political rise of Villelle, who became President of the Council in 1822. Villelle was apparently the ghost-writer of Mme du Cayla's daily letter to the King (**65**).

The experiment of constitutional monarchy under the patronage of the Bourbons ultimately failed in the hands of Charles X, the bigoted brother of Louis XVIII, who succeeded to the throne in 1824. Faced with growing opposition in the Chamber of Deputies, Charles made a last-ditch attempt to reassert the royal prerogative. In the Ordinances of St Cloud of 1830 he reduced the size of the electorate by altering the voting qualifications and imposed rigorous press censorship. His high-handedness brought about the revolution of that year. Monarchy, however, still survived in the person of Louis Philippe, the former Duc d'Orléans. Metternich's fear that demands for liberal reform led automatically to revolution was apparently justified, as the revolution that brought down Charles X produced revolutionary shock waves throughout the rest of Europe. It led to the first revision of the Vienna settlement with the establishment of the new kingdom of Belgium, entirely independent of Dutch rule. There were also revolutionary outbreaks in some of the German states. In Brunswick, Duke Karl II was forced to abdicate and his successor, Duke William, granted a constitution; reformed constitutions were also established in Saxony, Hanover and Hesse-Kassel. But the basic political structure of the Restoration remained intact in the German states as it did elsewhere, in the Italian peninsula and the Habsburg lands. Nonetheless, the changes in France and Belgium caused the monarchs of Europe to be more watchful, and none more so than Louis Philippe, whose government had to suppress a major insurrection at Lyon in 1834.

Theoretically the government of Louis Philippe was constitutional, in that his authority was to be restrained by representative institutions. In practice considerable power still lay with the King, and like Louis XVIII and Charles X, Louis Philippe still had the power to initiate legislation personally. This meant that there was always the possibility of a conflict between the Chamber of Deputies and the King, since the Chamber was expected to debate and approve legislation presented to it by the King's chosen ministers. The conflict between the King's chosen minister, Guizot*, and the Chamber of Deputies became the most prominent political feature of the July Monarchy in the 1840s.

Other Europeans regarded France as an essentially liberal state. East of the Rhine, Europe was made up of a series of non-constitutional states where the kings and princes felt no need to justify their authority; in their view it was part of the natural order of things. For instance, with the restoration of the House of Savoy in the Kingdom of Piedmont-Sardinia in 1815, the new King Victor Emmanuel I threw the whole state into chaos with a single edict by refusing to recognise any law passed since 1777. The aristocracy again became exempt from taxation and the Church recovered its ancient rights (**171**). Autocracy in the Habsburg Empire was equally vigorous. In the years after 1815 the mechanism of repression for the maintenance of stability 'was developed into a fine art as never before' (**148**). Metternich believed that any form of constitutional concession which diluted the power of the monarchy was an invitation to extreme and revolutionary change. In January 1848 he wrote: 'The impending conflict will tear the mask from the face of reform to show it in all its horror as the spectre of radicalism' (**18**). Thus for Metternich liberal constitutional reform was a Trojan horse that would eventually bring down all the established institutions of the state.

There is a sense in which the decade beginning in 1830 marks a significant shift in terms of the political stability of Europe. The period 1815 to 1830 saw conservatism ascendant, with the ruling class exerting more or less effective control. Increasingly, after 1830, new political forces which were corrosive of the existing political order began to emerge. These new forces can be categorised under four headings: liberalism, democracy, socialism and nationalism.

Liberalism in the nineteenth century was the belief that government should be carried on with the consent of the various sections of society or the nation. Liberalism's intellectual justification was derived from eighteenth-century rationalism, which had attacked all forms of arbitrary authority, particularly that of kings. Liberals believed that the power of traditional institutions, such as the Church and the monarchy, should be restrained by new institutions representing the interests of society more generally and the aristocracy and the wealthier sections of the middle class in particular. The liberal programme – government by parliament or representative assembly, freedom of the press and individual freedom – was popular among the emerging classes of manufacturers, merchants and professionals, who saw the privileges of the Church and the most wealthy sections of the aristocracy as obstacles to their own economic and social improvement. Thus alongside demands for distinctly political reforms, liberalism also embraced demands for economic freedom – free trade and the abolition of tariffs, together with the erosion of feudal restrictions. The emergence of liberalism, then, was often synonymous with the emergence of the middle class and with economic development and progress. Liberals, as distinct from democrats, believed in the sovereignty of parliament, rather than the sovereignty of the people. Middle-class liberals regarded democracy with suspicion, since it was associated in their minds with the excesses of the French First Republic. Consequently, middle-class liberals in both Britain and France advocated broadening the property franchise. They did not advocate universal male suffrage: '*Vox populi, vox dei*, which gives to the majority the infallibility of God . . . is the most despotic absurdity that has ever emerged from the human brain. If you want to ruin a state give universal suffrage'. So claimed Odilon Barrot, leader of the Dynastic Opposition* in the French Chamber of Deputies in the 1840s (quoted in **18**). A similar view was expressed by the Piedmontese politician Camillo Cavour, who said in 1847, 'No people should be electors unless their income and intelligence indicated that they . . . had a vested interest in social order. Ideally the electorate should be the mercantile classes, the professions and especially the owners of land' (quoted in **168**).

Liberal   political   campaigns   had   as   their   objective   the establishment or strengthening of the parliamentary system of government. In France in the 1840s, this took the form of a demand for broadening the franchise to admit greater numbers of the middle classes into political life. The campaign had been initiated in the Chamber by Barrot and Adolphe Thiers but was later taken up outside parliament by the publisher Laurent-Antoine Paguerre, in May 1847. He was the dominant figure of the *Comité Central des Électeurs de la Seine*, which had orginally been set up in the 1846 election to organise opposition candidates to Guizot's* supporters. It was from this originally modest movement that the campaign of the Banqueteers developed as an archetypal example of liberal middle-class expression. The first political banquet was held on 9 July 1847, and it was addressed by Paguerre and Barrot. Thiers refused to participate as he regarded the banquets as invitations to political extremism and demagoguery. He was proved correct, as the banquets were taken over by republican politicians demanding democratic reforms. The campaign of the Banqueteers was in some ways similar to the campaign of the Anti-Corn Law League in Britain, which was also a typical expression of middle-class liberalism.

Elsewhere on the Continent, with the important exception of Belgium, liberalism made little headway. In the German states it was simply part of an academic debate among various German professors. The 1830 revolutions undoubtedly gave this debate a renewed impetus. Between 1834 and 1844 Professors Rotteck and Welcker at Freiburg University produced a number of works on liberalism, and in 1835 Dahlmann published his famous *Politik*. Younger writers, for example Heine, were also attracted to liberalism and a festival was held at Hambach in 1832 to discuss liberal ideas. It caused great alarm in ruling circles and Metternich successfully persuaded the German *Diet* to introduce press censorship and fresh controls on the universities. In the Habsburg lands liberal ideas began to be debated in the later 1830s. In Vienna the Legal-Political Reading Club was founded in 1842: its members were prominent bourgeois intellectuals, such as Alexander Bach*, Schmerling and Doblhoff. They developed a reform programme which demanded the abolition of the feudal labour rent known as the *Robot**, the establishment of a representative parliament, the submission of the state budget to parliamentary approval and a general reform of the taxation system. Elsewhere within the Habsburg territories the discussion of liberalism was most advanced in Hungary and Lombardy, perhaps the two most economically developed parts of the Empire at this time. In Hungary a liberal aristocrat, Stephen

Szechenyi*, published a series of works between 1828 and 1833 advocating economic reforms, including the abolition of peasant feudal obligations, and his ideas were no doubt formative in encouraging the Hungarian *Diet* to petition the monarchy in 1829 to abolish the restrictive tariffs which so hampered Hungary's commerce. A similar economic liberalism also developed in Lombardy, where the journalist Romagnosi advocated various reforms designed to encourage commercial development. Cattaneo also published many articles advocating liberal measures. As yet, much of this liberal discussion was little more than an intellectual debate. It had not become a coherent political programme with sizeable support. Yet although the number of men involved in the discussions was small, they were located in the major cities which formed the *loci* of political power. The liberals remained a minority, but their presence in Paris, Vienna, Budapest, Milan and Berlin gave them a significance disproportionate to their numbers.

Early nineteenth-century democrats advocated universal male suffrage as a means of securing a government which would express the general will of the people. Ultimately, therefore, democrats were republicans, as they believed in the abolition of monarchy and hereditary power. It was these ideas that had motivated the Jacobins in France and had led to the execution of Louis XVI in 1793. Democracy continued to appeal to the urban working class in the early nineteenth century, and some republicans made a conscious appeal to this section of society: 'To the workers! To their indefeasible rights, to their sacred interests, up to the present unrecognised', declared Ledru-Rollin at a political banquet in Lille in 1847. However, the attitude of bourgeois republican politicians towards the rights of the working class was often ambivalent. The possibility of a repetition of the excesses of the Revolutionary Terror of 1792 was something that lingered in the minds of the respectable classes. Thus, although Ledru-Rollin was seen as the reincarnation of Robespierre by the *noblesse* and the *grande bourgeoisie*, as Minister of the Interior in the Second Republic in 1848 he was less enthusiastic about workers' rights. When the people of Paris invaded the Chamber of Deputies in May 1848, Ledru-Rollin no doubt saw the spectre of mob rule, and it was this that prompted him to call for order; de Tocqueville*, in describing the scene, said that Ledru-Rollin was 'hooted down' and forced to leave the rostrum (**7**).

Apparently, then, even radical politicians like Ledru-Rollin believed that parliament came before the will of the people. But how widespread was the attraction of democracy in early nineteenth-century Europe? Democratic politics were most developed in France, where the traditions of the first Revolution gave democratic government a working precedent, and also in the Italian states, as well as among exiled Poles. The *Manifesto* of the Polish Democratic Society had been published in Paris in 1836 and there was a democratic strain in the Polish national movement (**175**). In France democracy had continued to gain ground after 1815 despite the reactionary politics of the Restoration. The 1816 Education Decree which had ordered the establishment of a school in every commune, so that by 1820 24,000 out of 44,000 communes had schools, undoubtedly facilitated the politicisation of the people (**60**). Associated with this development was the increase in the number of teacher-training colleges – *écoles normales* – from twelve to forty-seven between 1833 and 1848 (**72**). The growing class of elementary-school teachers often found themselves in the democratic republican camp. In provincial France these new school-teachers provided a new source of knowledge and authority that was contrary to that provided by the village priest. In many of the provincial cities of France – Lyon, Toulon, Limoges, for example – the *petite bourgeoisie* were often found in the republican vanguard. There were a small number of republican deputies in the Chamber before 1848 – Ledru-Rollin, Arago, Carnot and Marie – who 'constituted a possible pole of attraction for those deputies who were moving away from the regime'(**60**). The process of spreading republican ideas was also promoted, of course, by the growth of the press, which appealed to an increasingly literate population. *Le National* was the most important republican newspaper during the period of the July Monarchy, and there were also a number of republican journals such as the *Revue Indépendante* founded by George Sand and Pierre Leroux. The spread of literacy was considerable and it has been estimated that the proportion of conscripts recruited from the district of the Var – these would mostly have been peasants – who could read and write increased from 33 per cent in 1831 to 60 per cent by 1851 (**61**). Whilst literacy should not be thought a prerequisite for the spread of political vocabulary and ideas, it certainly helped.

On the Italian peninsula, democratic organisations had been established in a number of Italian cities, and almost all the middle-class intellectuals who became involved in the democratic movement were from urban backgrounds (**165**). Italy's ancient urban tradition, and the fact that the towns were traditionally seen as centres of learning as well as centres of government, helped this development. Not only were there democratic organisations in the larger cities such as Milan, Turin, Genoa and Florence, but there were also organisations in the smaller centres including Mantua, Pisa, Lucca and Livorno. However, these democratic clubs were purely localised and no democratic leader, probably not even Mazzini*, could 'claim to be a nationally-known figure' (**165**). Much of the activity of the republican-democrats was confined to café discussions and the reading of banned newspapers. There were, however, a number of attempts at revolutionary uprisings – at Bologna in 1843, Naples in 1844 and Romagna in 1845; and in this way the democrats 'kept the cauldron of Italian politics bubbling' (**165**).

Those who argued that some kind of social reform or change in the economic organisation of society was necessary over and above political reform were, in the 1830s and 1840s, called socialists. Socialism was not at this time a precisely defined doctrine. Indeed, its development as a clearly articulated ideology was still only in its infancy. The term 'socialist' had been used first by Robert Owen, the English philanthropist, in the *Co-operative Magazine* of 1827 (**32**). His thinking about economics owed much to Adam Smith, but was at the same time infused with moral notions about the just deserts of labour. Owen claimed that the value of any commodity was determined by the present and past labour that had gone into it, since past labour had produced existing capital or stock. These ideas were to be explained and extended in more scientific terms by Ricardo and, more significantly for subsequent history, by Karl Marx. If the value of a commodity was determined by the amount of present and past labour involved in producing it, then the key question, Owen claimed, was whether capital, the accumulation of the efforts of labour over time, should be individually or commonly owned or controlled. From this he derived the basis of socialism: namely, the common ownership of the means of production, distribution and exchange.

The great problem that faced those who believed that common ownership was socially just was how to achieve their ends. Many people who were called socialists in the 1840s may have advocated social reform, philanthropy or co-operation along the lines sketched out by Owen. In France, however, the common ownership of the 'fruits of the earth' was, for some men, only to be achieved by violent insurrection. Here was a fusion of a revolutionary tradition with ideas of social as well as political equality. Foremost in the conspiratorial revolutionary tradition in France in the 1830s and 1840s were the secret societies inspired by Auguste Blanqui*. It was to this revolutionary tradition that Marx and Engels referred in their

Communist Manifesto produced in 1848. Writing much later, Engels observed that it would have been impossible to write a 'Socialist Manifesto', since socialism was the theory of respectable middle-class doctrinaires. The word 'communism', however, was far from respectable, as it carried connotations of insurrection and militancy [**doc. 2f**].

Between those whom Marx and Engels regarded as middle-class doctrinaires and social reformers, like Owen in England and Charles Fourier in France, and the advocates of proletarian revolution, such as themselves, stood those who saw the state as capable of dispensing social justice. Louis Blanc* was probably the most important advocate of this strategy and he was to play an important role in the Provisional Government formed in France after the abdication of Louis Philippe. Blanc believed that the state should regulate the economy – an idea derived from Saint-Simon* – and that it should guarantee the 'right to work'. Blanc was in fact adopting what was later to become the basis of social democracy – the belief that socialist reforms could be achieved democratically through the election of socialist representatives – which was quite distinct from the revolutionary or communist stance adopted by Blanqui* and Marx.

How widely were socialist ideas accepted or even discussed? The short answer is probably very little. The diffusion of socialist ideas and the extent to which the working class were attracted to socialism has prompted much debate among historians (**20, 62, 81, 89, 107**), and the most complete analyses are those that have tried to tie the issues of changing social structure to worker 'consciousness' and ideology (see above, pp. 10–12). It seems likely that educated artisans were most likely to be attracted to socialism. Artisans were very much to the fore in socialist-inspired protest movements in centres of old craft production such as Lyon, Lodève and Tours (**75, 89**). Admittedly there were instances where artisans continued to be attracted to royalist political traditions – in Toulouse and Marseille, for example (**62, 107**). But wherever the culture and economy of the artisans were threatened in absolute or relative terms their sense of 'community and professional pride made them the vanguard of worker resistance movements' (**75**). This would also seem to have been the case elsewhere. In the German states the *Handwerker* were politically active in old craft centres such as Krefeld and Elberfeld (**111**); and in Italy it was the artisans in Milan, Venice, Rome and Palermo who were most politically aware (**172**).

Overall, the general political activity enveloped under the heading 'socialism' was extremely diverse. Consequently, socialism as an ideological force that motivated men in the 1848 revolutions should not be overestimated. It was probably more significant in France than anywhere else on the Continent. Liberalism and democracy, and particularly the former in the minds of the rising middle class, were much more potent political ideas immediately before 1848, primarily because liberalism had had some measure of success in France, Britain and Belgium. The success of liberalism was perhaps the most sensitive barometer of middle-class dynamism. Middle-class achievement and the progress of liberalism went hand in hand. An equally powerful political belief, especially east of the Rhine, was nationalism.

Nationalists believed that a group of people who shared a common language, history, heritage, culture and possibly religion, should be brought together to form nation states [**docs 2b, c**]. Britain and France were already nation states in this sense. After 1815 those who hoped to form a national Italy or a national Germany were for the most part liberal, since the constitution of a nation state involved consent within society about a form of government. Nationalism had at first been given great impetus by Jacobin ideas of democracy. Obviously the concept of 'sovereignty of the people' could be construed as a nationalist idea as well as a democratic one, since presumably 'a people' would have to unite in order to achieve sovereignty. Moreover, the Napoleonic conquests provoked a sense of nationalism in those parts of Europe that came within the French Empire, especially the Confederation of the Rhine and the Italian States. However, the excesses of the Revolutionary Terror tended to discredit democracy; consequently after 1815 nationalism was increasingly associated with liberalism.

Modern nationalism had its origins in the eighteenth century. It had been carried into central and southern Europe by Napoleon. At the same time, central European intellectuals began to articulate nationalist ideas. In Germany, for example, Johann Herder advanced the notion of *Volkgeist* or 'national soul', by which he meant a consciousness that produced a particular language, art and culture, particular attitudes to life, customs and traditions. Not surprisingly, therefore, the early stirrings of nationalism manifested themselves in the activities of the middle classes and the gentry and more specifically the educated elite [**doc. 2c**]. Historical writing in particular was a means of establishing national identity: the Czech historian, Frantisek Palacky, was at work on a history of Bohemia before 1848, and in 1842 Szafarzik published his *Slavonic Ethnography*. In Italy the historical novels of Alessandro Manzoni recalled the past greatness of Italy, but obviously appealed only to a literate minority.

In the German states nationalism was enmeshed in the liberal movement generally and centred in the universities. The German professors, Dahlmann and Welcker, were the articulate spokesmen of the German national idea. From 1840 onwards German liberal-nationalists increasingly began to look towards Prussia as the state most capable of uniting the German people. In that year Frederick William IV came to the throne and he seemed disposed to both liberalism and nationalism. A political amnesty was granted and a number of academics were reinstated; most notably the brothers Grimm were given teaching posts in Berlin, having been dismissed from Gottingen in 1837 (**111**). Professionals were at the forefront in promoting the national tradition. Societies of philologists were established in Frankfurt in 1846 and Lubeck in 1847. Throughout the 1840s many German towns and cities established choral societies that promoted German music and patriotic songs. This cultivation of a national cultural and artistic tradition provided a vital cement for holding together national political movements.

The various national movements within the Habsburg Empire were complex and diverse. Magyar nationalism was the most vigorous and Szechenyi's* economic writings had done much to establish the notion of Magyar economic primacy within the Empire. Further, the Habsburg system of government already recognised the Hungarian identity by allowing the Hungarians their own provincial *Diet*. Inadvertently, therefore, the Habsburgs gave the emergent generation of Hungarian political spokesmen a platform on which to articulate their programme. Lajos Kossuth was the leading figure in this campaign. He had been arrested in 1837 but released in 1839 on Metternich's advice. On his release, Kossuth began editing *Pesti Hirlap*, a Magyar journal, and it soon reached a circulation of 10,000. Magyar nationalism was ambitious and its stridency implied Magyar claims to rule other minorities in the eastern part of the Empire. Thus other nationalist movements in Croatia and Transylvania were not always anti-Habsburg; they were often anti-Magyar. In Zagreb, for example, Ljudevit Gaj founded the *Croat News* in 1835, claiming that he hoped to influence opinion among the Croats and Slovenes 'against Hungary's purpose of achieving independence'. In Transylvania, too, Romanian nationalism had a distinctly anti-Magyar tinge.

The diversity of national ambition among the subject peoples of the Empire was ultimately a great strength for the Habsburgs, since resentment of Habsburg rule could thereby be diffused. After all, it was the Croatian Josef Jellacic who helped save the Empire by suppressing Kossuth's independent Hungarian Republic in 1849. Elsewhere in the Empire nationalism followed a similar form to that displayed in the German states. In Prague, for example, Czech intellectuals promoted social events where Czech was spoken, most famously the Czech Ball of February 1840. Traditionally German had been the official written language of the Bohemian lands of the Habsburg Empire, but Palacky had already set up the Czech Foundation in 1831 to encourage the publication of Czech books. Czech nationalism was part of the general Slavic renaissance: the Slovak poet, Jan Kollar, did much to inspire a consciousness of Slavic traditions in the 1820s, and the Polish Revolution of 1831 had a similar impact on Slavic nationalism generally (**148, 151**).

In Italy the nationalist movement was an outgrowth of a general cultural renaissance, or *Risorgimento*. The *Risorgimento* provided the intellectual springs of Italian nationalism which was directed primarily against the Habsburgs. The Settlement of 1815 had made the Habsburg Empire the most extensive and powerful territorial unit in central-southern Europe. The extent of the Empire meant that Metternich's principal task was the handling of many subject peoples. Thus the Italians of Lombardy and Venetia saw Italian nationalism in terms of establishing their independence from the Habsburgs. Elsewhere in the peninsula nationalists were more concerned about the problem of welding the various independent states into a single national unit. The Italian national movement was extremely diverse. Mazzini's* republican nationalism vied with Gioberti's* vision of a federation of Italian states under the presidency of the Pope; and there were also the ideas of economic federalism advocated by Romagnosi, which no doubt owed something to the example of the German *Zollverein*. Ultimately, the most realistic programme for unification that emerged before 1846 was that put forward by D'Azeglio*, a leading liberal politician in Piedmont. D'Azeglio advocated a federation of Italian states under Piedmontese leadership, and in the long run it was, in fact, the economic and military primacy of Piedmont which determined the nature of Italian unification.

The important point to remember about nationalism in the years before 1848 is that it was still in its embryonic stage. Nationalists were unable to co-ordinate their diverse programmes. The protracted discussions of the members of the Frankfurt Assembly are proof of this point (see pp. 83–4). Nonetheless, all the political ideas that have been discussed – liberalism, democracy, socialism and nationalism – were new forces gnawing away at the stability of existing political structures. The ruling classes regarded them all as dangerous, but very often proved incapable of effectively suppressing them, particularly as the economic condition of Europe underwent dramatic changes in the 1840s. It is here that some of the most difficult problems in analysing the causes of the 1848 revolutions are to be found. Most historians have stressed the lack of coherence that existed within the revolutionary movements, and explanations of the failures of the revolutions rely heavily on this kind of argument (**26, 42**).

Yet the European governments were often gripped with a kind of paralysis when faced with the initial revolutionary outbreaks. There are two sharply divergent schools of thought on this point. Marxist historians stress the importance of economic factors in mobilising the immiserated sections of the population who, living on the margins of existence, were driven to spontaneous uprising by the financial and food crises of 1846–47. In this explanation there is often a gap between ideological development – liberalism, nationalism and democracy in particular – which had apparently been so corrosive of the existing order in the twenty years before 1848, and the motives of those who took to the barricades. It seems almost contradictory that the revolutions were made by those classes who were least touched by the general range of liberal ideologies. For the Marxist historians the key point is that it was primarily the working classes who died on the barricades:

> In Berlin there were only about fifteen [middle-class] representatives, about thirty master craftsmen among the three hundred victims of the March fighting; in Milan, only twelve students, white-collar workers or landlords among the 350 dead of the insurrection. It was their hunger [i.e. the poor] which powered the demonstrations that turned into revolution (**23**).

This type of explanation rests on the assumption that social and economic factors were of prime importance in the 1848 revolutions. The second type of explanation, however, tends to concentrate on the failure of governments to come to terms with the challenges that they faced. This argument stresses the almost accidental factors which derived from the inadequacy of particular rulers. Guizot* was unpopular, inflexible and blind to the troubles that were on the horizon; Frederick William IV of Prussia acted rashly and did not heed his political advisers; Metternich was no longer able to act with the certainty he had displayed in his younger days; while Pope Pius IX raised expectations by granting liberal reforms at an unpropitious moment. Thus Peter Stearns argues that 'unready governments, headed by indecisive rulers . . . facilitated the conversion of street fighting into full-scale revolution' (**42**). The details of this interpretation will be understood more fully by examining events in individual countries (see below, pp. 52–97), but this kind of approach clearly stresses the failure of the elite. 'Weakness and confusion at the top . . . were vital to the causation of the revolutions of 1848. Where regimes remained confident revolutions did not occur. In Britain the government was sufficiently sure of itself to make concessions to middle-class demands and thereby begin the process of forming a new ruling elite' (**42**). This argument has a certain attraction and it does of course act as a counterpoint to explanations which stress the primacy of the economic crisis in releasing irresistible forces that swept governments aside (**55, 73**). However, the elite-failure argument raises two important questions. First, if the rulers were incompetent why had regimes in the past survived with equally incompetent rulers? Whole systems rarely cave in because of the shortcomings of a particular individual. There does seem to have been a collective *malaise* at the top and a sense of fear that pervaded the ruling classes (**7**). The second question is why were the ruling classes so frightened? The answer is that they did not live in a political vacuum. They were fearful of the new ideologies and they were horrified by the spectres of violence and disorder which emanated from the cities. It may be that the ruling classes overestimated the significance of the new ideologies, yet the fear which these inspired among them led to the collective paralysis of regimes on a wholesale basis. Revolutions are caused by a complex of issues and the interplay between the forces of change and the reactions of the champions of order is one of the most difficult problems that historians have to grapple with.

6   The Crisis of the 1840s

There is little doubt that the general economic condition of Europe deteriorated in the 1840s, especially in the period 1845–47. The precise nature of this deterioration, and therefore its effect on the different classes of the population, has been hotly disputed by historians. Even those who have stressed the importance of political factors in the causes of the revolutions have accepted that 'there is a close relationship between the political crisis which culminated in the overthrow of the July Monarchy and the economic crisis which marked its final years' (**72**). However, it should be remembered that all revolutions are essentially political, whereas not all economic crises result in revolutions. The social unrest that ensues from economic catastrophe must become channelled into political activity that challenges the validity of existing institutions (**71**). What, then, was the nature of the economic catastrophe in Europe in the 1840s? Simply put, the widespread agricultural crisis caused by crop failures brought rapid increases in grain and bread prices [**docs 4a–c**]. The hardships caused by the price increases were further compounded by the effects of a potato blight which drastically affected the standard of living of the working classes in the towns and the peasantry in the countryside. Whether this was a crucial and decisive cause of the revolutions historians now doubt. Food riots alone do not lead to revolutions.

There was also a financial and industrial crisis, especially in France. Its effect was to depress the confidence of the investing classes. Additionally, it brought about an increase in unemployment in the manufacturing towns of Lille, Roubaix, Tourcoing and Mulhouse, where many textile mills were forced to close. But again it must be stressed that it is difficult to trace the effect of these economic disasters on political events.

It makes sense to look at the agricultural crisis first, since changes in food prices affected the poor, the majority of the population, most profoundly. Remembering that approximately 70 per cent of working-class income was spent on food at this time, rises in the price of grain products in the region of 100 to 150 per cent in the space of two years had a devastating effect on the condition of a class whose existence was already precarious. Price rises were especially marked in France, but there were dramatic increases elsewhere. For instance, the price of wheat in Hamburg rose by 60 per cent between 1845 and 1847. There was a similar increase in the cost of rye. The wretched condition of the workers in the German states was also attested to by contemporaries, as in the case of J. J. Dittrich, who claimed in 1847: 'Not a small number of the inhabitants of the province which is called the pearl of the crown of Prussia, Silesia, live far worse than the convicts of the prisons' (**29**). It is also important to look at the price of other starch foods which formed such a substantial part of the diet of the poor, particularly potatoes. The price of potatoes in some German towns increased by as much as 135 per cent between 1846 and 1847, and there is no doubt that the lower classes in the towns and in the countryside became increasingly impoverished and demoralised [**doc 3a**]. These deteriorating conditions often produced sporadic outbreaks of violence. In Konigsberg in Prussia, there were assaults on tax collectors; in the small town of Prokul an angry crowd demolished the courthouse and beat a local landowner to death (**143**). Similarly, in Liebstadt, rural labourers attacked the estate of a local landowner and demolished his house. In the northern territories of the Habsburg Empire there were devastating floods on the plain of the Vistula in which the homes of 60,000 peasants were destroyed. The subsequent price rises of staple grain products were catastrophic. The worst-hit areas were Bohemia and Silesia. In turn, the cities – principally Vienna but also Linz – became inundated with destitute peasants in search of charitable relief (**148**).

In Habsburg Venetia conditions were no better. The price of wheat in the Venice markets almost doubled between 1845 and 1847. The price of maize had risen from 11 Austrian lire in 1845 to 19.5 lire in 1847. In Polesine, wheat and maize prices had risen threefold in the period 1845–47. Conditions in the countryside of the Veneto sharply deteriorated after 1844. The harvest of 1845 was poor and that of 1846 was blighted by disease. Not surprisingly, the peasantry were driven to taking matters into their own hands. In February 1848 the villagers of Polesella on the River Po broke into local granaries and distributed the grain; and in the district of Treviso two merchants were stoned by a crowd at Pieve. In the village of Cazzano, near Verona, the local inhabitants forced the police to seek refuge for a whole day in the house of a local official (**174**). Matters in Venetia were no doubt exacerbated by maladministration on the part of the Habsburgs, who permitted the export of grain to England until well into 1848.

There were also food riots in the Low Countries, in Leyden, the Hague, Delft and Haarlem in 1845 (**51**). The effects of the potato blight were particularly acute in Belgium, causing extensive migrations of people into north-east France, which served only to intensify the problems of unemployment and put yet greater strain upon the resources of the charitable institutions in the region.

Conditions in France deserve special attention, since it was events in that country which have been thought to be so formative for the rest of the continent. The grain harvests were certainly patchy. In some regions in 1846 and 1847 they were quite good, notably in Haute-Garonne and Franche Comté: but in central France and the Midi the harvests were poor and peasant unrest in the wake of the ensuing food crisis was considerable. In Buzençais in the department of Indres local artisans and rural labourers acted together to halt grain convoys. Subsequently they sold off the grain at what was considered to be a just price. Crowds of townspeople pillaged flour mills and a local moneylender was killed. How bad the grain harvests in France were in the years immediately before 1848 is best appreciated by noting the increase in grain imports. In 1846 France imported grain to the value of 125 million francs. By the following year this had almost doubled to 231 million francs. The chief ports of entry for grain were Marseille and Arles; but the rail link from Paris to Marseille via Lyon was incomplete. Grain still had to be transported by steamer or barge along the Rhône. In 1843 the steamer journey from Arles to Lyon took thirty-five hours, whilst a barge took a month. This helps to explain the variation in the economic map of France and the widespread differences in the price of grain between the northern and central districts compared with the rest of France. In fact, the coastal regions were not significantly affected by food shortages (**55**). Nonetheless, the effects of the food crisis were extremely severe, debilitating vast sections of a population that was ill-equipped to face such a disaster.

The food crisis alone does not explain the revolution. In the first instance, there was probably little direct connection between the food riots instigated by peasants and rural artisans and the eventual collapse of governments. The food riots often occurred in rural areas or in towns and cities that were remote from the centres of political power. Rather, the food crisis had an indirect effect: it served to alarm the ruling elites, and thereby contributed to the paralysis of governments. Alarm at the extent of unrest may have undermined business confidence, primarily among the investing classes (**75**), who withdrew their funds. This in turn helped to set off another chain of social and economic problems. The fact remains, though, that the food riots were localised, sporadic and lacking in focus. The rioters had no intention of overthrowing governments. They had no political programme and their actions were directed against local tyrants – tax collectors, landlords and usurers. It should also be remembered that the harvest of 1847 was somewhat better than those of the previous two years, so that by the autumn of 1847 and the winter of 1848 food prices were beginning to fall, precisely at the moment when disorder broke out in the capital cities of Europe. The relationship between the food crisis and the political crisis of 1848 is therefore extremely difficult to establish in any obvious way. The food crisis certainly contributed to the breakdown of order during 1847 but it is doubtful whether, by itself, it acted as a detonator for the revolutions of the following year.

There were a number of factors that converged in the 1840s to intensify peasant distress, and one of its principal consequences was emigration. Many countrymen were pushed from the land and forced to seek new opportunities in the towns and cities. Some even made their way beyond Europe itself. The spread of the market economy and capitalist modes of production and organisation was uneven. In some regions of Europe peasant farmers were quasi-capitalists responding to market forces. This was particularly the case in the commercialised regions of viticulture such as Champagne and Burgundy. Elsewhere subsistence agriculture persisted – as in the Périgord, where peasant women foraged in the woods for chestnuts as a supplement to the staple diet of black bread. In the Limousin, peasants migrated to Paris and Lyon to work in the building and construction trades. The peasants of upland Aquitaine migrated to Languedoc. There was a long history of rural conflict over such matters as grazing, foraging in the feudal forests, and use of the common lands. Peasant frustration was increasingly vented against landowners, the forest guards, the tax collectors and the money-lenders. This was also the case in eastern Europe. In the countryside around Tilsit the local newspaper, the *Vossiche Zeitung*, lamented that the 'grossest excesses are being carried out against persons and property; the village Mayors are no longer respected, and are even abused; senseless demands are made on the land-owners, accompanied by the most dangerous threats from the lowest classes; taxes are withheld by entire villages' (**139**).

Distress in the countryside also rebounded upon the towns. The impact of migration upon Paris was especially marked, for it significantly increased the rate at which the population was expanding. In 1817 Paris had just over 700,000 inhabitants; by 1846 it had well over a million. The increase of population between 1841 and 1846 was 12.56 per cent, with immigration being significantly higher in this period than it had been earlier. The majority of the immigrants were itinerant, and depended upon lodging-houses for accommodation. In 1831 the lodging-house population stood at 23,150 but by 1846 it had increased to 50,007 (**64**). By far the largest section of this itinerant population was male and young, and therefore constituted a vast pool of potentially violent rioters. There was already a long tradition of violence in an urban environment that had been deteriorating throughout the period 1830–46, due to a vast increase in the population and a decline in the available stock of housing. This set of circumstances may explain why the Parisian proletariat took to the streets and challenged the existing order in 1848 (**40, 64**). But such a claim should be made with caution and set against the counterpoint that the forces of order and control lacked cohesiveness as well as sufficient conviction to carry out an effective suppression (see Chapter 5).

The second major aspect of the economic crisis of the 1840s was the financial and industrial collapse. The food crisis and the financial-industrial crisis interacted with one another and also had a cumulative impact upon society. Again, events in France deserve special attention. In 1841 Guizot's* government had passed a statute facilitating the compulsory purchase of land for the purpose of railway building. The government had established the principle that the state should share the cost with private enterprise. Railways were certainly needed both economically and militarily, and railway matters took up much debating time in the Chamber of Deputies. Government intervention in this area was also a means of attracting foreign capital. English banks were particularly active, but from 1845, owing to the problems of British industry at that time, they followed a policy of sale and liquidation which caused a sharp decline in share values. Government backing for railway investment had also encouraged speculation in metallurgical industries. There was a vast increase in iron output, which resulted in overproduction, and in 1847 iron production fell by about 30 per cent. Coal production also shrank by 20 per cent. The final crisis in confidence was reflected in massive falls of share prices on the Bourse. Since the government had itself invested over 600 million francs in railways, road construction and the rebuilding of the fortifications of Paris, these developments created a crisis of confidence. The press was quick to seize upon this: 'It is the government which has precipitated this condition of ruin' (**55**). The financial crisis and the associated problems of over-production also caused unemployment. This rose to 35 per cent among metal workers and 20 per cent among miners, and was especially concentrated in the north-east in the Lille-Tourcoing region. Industrial unemployment was compounded by growing rural unemployment. Capitalised agricultural regions had been shedding labour anyway. Further, when the prices of agricultural products began to fall at the end of 1847, farmers elected to cut their labour forces still further, as a means of sustaining the profit margins which had grown in the period of rising prices.

The financial crisis also directly affected the business classes, especially those sections whose credit resources were limited. In 1845 there had been 691 bankruptcies in Paris; between April 1846 and July 1847 there were 1,139. These bankruptcies were largely concentrated among shopkeepers and wholesale merchants – members of the *petite bourgeoisie*. They were being forced out of business by larger businessmen who, being denied export opportunities abroad, especially in Britain, began dumping their products at lower prices on the home market.

It was this crisis in the *petite bourgeoisie*, rather than unemployment among the workers or the hunger of the masses, that was probably decisive in the Paris revolution. The National Guard, a kind of volunteer police force, recruited considerable numbers of its members from this class and it was the defection of National Guardsmen to the side of the protesters that prompted Louis Philippe to dispense with his favoured minister, Guizot*. Thus the alienation from the government of a section of society that was traditionally loyal to the regime was of crucial significance in turning a protest into a revolution. The interaction of the financial crisis with existing political discontent is a complex matter, as was demonstrated by the Banqueteers campaign. The banquet campaign was especially popular amongst the members of the *petite bourgeoisie* as it gave them an opportunity to vent their ill-feeling towards the monarchy. Thus, although the regime nominally represented the interest of the middle classes, in reality it only promoted the interests of the *haute bourgeoisie*. These divisions had been present from the beginning of the July Monarchy – 'From now on the bankers will rule', claimed the liberal banker Lafitte in July 1830 – but they had seemed less important during the period of rising expectations between 1830 and 1845. Once the economic boom had petered out, however, the 'deep fissures in the propertied classes' (**75**) became all too apparent and the narrow basis of the regime's support became manifest. Issues that might, on other occasions, have seemed of little significance suddenly became extremely divisive.

What was beginning to happen was that groups who were normally loyal to the regime were becoming increasingly intolerant of it. Whether this should be attributed primarily to the financial crisis or to other developments is a matter of debate, but there is no doubt that the groups to whom Louis Philippe would previously have looked for support were no longer prepared to give it. De Tocqueville* claimed that the regime was overthrown because of the 'contempt into which the governing class . . . had fallen', a contempt so general and profound that it paralysed the resistance even of those who were most interested in maintaining the power that was being overthrown. Numerous instabilities – political, economic and social – coincided (**55**).

The financial crisis was not confined to France. In Germany, a depression in the textile industry resulted in a 40 per cent fall in the export of unbleached yarn from the *Zollverein* states between 1844 and 1847 (**116**). In fact there was a general overproduction problem in many of Germany's industrial centres; and financial institutions were often on the brink of collapse – the Abraham Schaaffhausen bank, in Cologne, was only saved from collapse when the Prussian government converted many of its assets into shares (**14**). In Italy, especially in the northern commercial cities, there were severe financial problems and Frederico Oexle, a prominent Venetian businessman, was forced to suspend payments (**163**). Habsburg industry had been in difficulties since 1844, especially in Bohemia, and imperial tax revenues fell sharply between 1844 and 1847, which was no doubt due to the general downturn in economic activity on all fronts. In Vienna, fear of a war of intervention, instigated by Metternich to suppress revolution abroad, prompted the Viennese investors to withdraw their savings. The panic and subsequent run on the banks caused some merchant banking houses to cease trading (**148**). The imperial government was already heavily in debt and there were insufficient reserves to withstand the crisis.

The severity of the trade depressions served to stimulate the growing appetite for political change among the European middle classes. In France the *petite bourgeoisie* became more and more attracted to democratic republicanism. In the German states, businessmen and professional men demanded a stake in political life. In the Habsburg Empire and the Italian peninsula the middle classes were attracted to nationalism. The spectre of disorder, in the wake of the agricultural and industrial crises which stalked both town and countryside, paralysed the ruling elites. The revolution in Paris was, according to Zeldin, the least bloody of all the revolutions that had occurred in the city – only 350 people were killed and 500 were admitted to hospital. The defection of the National Guard was obviously of great importance; but of paramount significance was Louis Philippe's impotence. He allowed the 'sceptre to slip from his hand', as Louis Blanc* so aptly put it. The great power of the working class – more apparent than real as time proved – persuaded the established ruling classes to surrender their authority with little fight in the early months of 1848. Whether the rulers at this time were particularly weak or ineffective compared with rulers in other historical situations could provide a lengthy but probably fruitless discussion. More likely, historical circumstances – the agricultural crisis, the financial and industrial depression and the threat of widespread disorder – produced a mood of defeatism among the ruling elites precisely because they were encountering so many calamities at once. The threat of disorder was everywhere and this was well recognised by contemporaries. Guizot* chose not to act on the warnings of his prefects, believing that conditions would eventually improve, and for this he has been much criticised (**72**). Elsewhere the agents of the governments did act, as in the case of Radetzky*, who occupied Ferrara in 1847 as a pre-emptive measure. With hindsight this action has been seen as provocative. But Radetzky's own letters clearly show the reasons for his decision: 'my information from the provinces, though slight, is very alarming, for the whole country is in revolt and even the peasants are armed' (**168**).

The almost voluntary capitulation of the governments created a political vacuum that enabled hitherto politically and socially underprivileged classes – the workers and the lower middle class – to take the stage and compete for power. Although certain types of causes are more relevant in some places than others – the financial crisis was probably more important in France than in the Habsburg lands – the widespread nature of the revolutions obliges the historian to search for general explanations. The great common denominator was the city, for the cities were the centres of political power and they were also the *loci* of all the cumulative economic and social disorders which had racked the 1840s. The problems of population growth, immigration, the breakdown of urban services, all piled up in the cities where a dangerous cocktail fermented into which numerous social classes, all disenchanted, poured their potent contributions. It was in the cities that political exiles were to be found; indeed Mazzini* had established the League of Exiles in Paris in 1834. It was in the cities that national and liberal aspirations were voiced through a growing newspaper and pamphlet press. The inability of the ruling classes to control these cities effectively in a period of rapid change provides a major part of the explanation of the 1848 revolutions.

Part Three: 1848: The Year of Revolution

The fact that the revolutions of 1848 were so widespread has tempted historians to seek explanations that demonstrate the common themes of the revolutions, and at the same time to try and find all-embracing explanations. It is no longer sufficient to say that the rest of Europe merely followed France. This does not imply that the events in Paris were not of significance to the revolutionaries of Berlin, Milan and Vienna. But mere imitation does not in itself provide a satisfactory explanation. For one thing, it devalues the significance of events which took place outside France. Consequently, historical investigation has sought to explain the widespread nature of the revolutions by focusing on the broad-based problems that Europe was facing by the 1840s – the food crisis, the financial crisis, the general demand for liberal modes of government. But the more the revolutions are studied in detail, the more historians have had to concede that there were often causes that were peculiar and special to individual revolutions. Parisians, Berliners, Milanese and Venetians were often fighting local and specific campaigns and it would be bad history that sought to impose common patterns of behaviour that were not there. At the same time it would be an abdication of the historian's responsibility if he did not seek to find those common traits if they did exist. The pattern of events in Europe as a whole can only be understood by a more detailed examination of the developments that took place in individual states.

7   France

By the 1840s the Orleanist regime which had triumphed over Legitimate Monarchy in 1830 was losing credibility in the eyes of those who were active in political life. In January 1848, Enfantin wrote, 'The King is no longer young, the Chambers and government are both somewhat corrupt. . . . It seems to me that if it were not for this uneasiness, then financially and economically we would not be in a dangerous position.' Enfantin's observations hardly seem to imply that revolution was imminent. However, the scale of the social crisis in the countryside (see above, pp. 45–7) had alarmed many notables, and the prefect of Loir-et-Cher reported, in January 1847, that near Indre 'the wealthy inhabitants are leaving their residences and taking up refuge in the town' (**71**). Guizot's* government faced opposition, but this opposition – led by Barrot and Thiers – sought reform, not revolution. Indeed, one historian has made the pertinent comment that the campaign of the Banqueteers failed since the outcome of its activities was revolution and not reform (**72**). If this was the case it is important to identify the grievances of the reformers and trace the themes of their campaign.

Guizot* had dominated French politics since 1840 and the electoral victory of 1846 had seemingly entrenched his position and at least temporarily demoralised his opponents. But this victory was also, paradoxically, a fundamental political cause of Guizot's* downfall, as it induced complacency and blinded him to the storm clouds that were on the horizon. Opponents of the government were only temporarily quietened by the election of 1846. The opposition took up the cry of corruption. A particular grievance was the practice of Deputies obtaining official posts – there were 184 paid government officials in the Chamber prior to the elections of 1846 and only forty of these were known to vote against the government. There were also a number of scandals in high places – for example, the *affaire Petit*, which concerned a former government official who claimed that he had achieved the resignation of other officials by bribes. There had already been some embarrassment over the case of the Duc de Praslin, who was believed to have murdered his wife for the love of his children's English governess. There was also the case of Teste, who admitted using his position as Minister of Public Works to obtain personal business advantage. Other scandals came to light and the *Gazette des tribunaux* specialised in detailed reporting which shocked the *petite bourgeoisie* who adopted a high moral tone and were becoming increasingly alienated from the regime. Their alienation was indicated by the reluctance of the National Guard, largely recruited from the *petite bourgeoisie*, to suppress outbreaks of disorder in many of the larger towns (**71**). In short, the effect of these cases of corruption was to bring the governing classes into disrepute (**65**) and to throw Guizot's* ministry on to the 'defensive' (71).

Guizot* had also been subject to attack because of his apparent lack of dynamism in foreign affairs. Guizot's foreign policy had as its principal objective an improvement in relations with England, and he blocked demands from Dubergier de Hauranne for vigorous colonial wars. Guizot calculated, probably quite correctly, that such wars were likely to arouse English hostility, but inside France his approach was construed as timid and unpatriotic. Even in those areas where it might be claimed that the government made some innovative headway – in the field of public education and the promotion of railway building – there still seemed to be aspects of the policies that detracted from its achievement. Thus although the number of public education places provided under the Orleanist regime greatly increased – from 1.9 million in 1833 to 3.5 million in 1847 – the newly emergent class of elementary-school teachers were resentful of their low salaries. Arguably, the government's intervention in the field of railway building was one of its greatest achievements. The law of 1842 had established the principle of public loans as a means of financing railway building, and by 1847 1800 kilometres of track were open and a further 2800 were under construction. Yet the government's commitment in this area had the unintended effect of contributing to overproduction in the coal and iron sectors, which in turn compounded the financial crisis (see above, pp. 47–9). This latter misfortune was crucial in turning a middle-class campaign for moderate reform into something which challenged the legitimacy of the regime itself.

From 1846 the growing impatience of the opposition in the Chamber of Deputies was becoming more apparent and in March and April 1847 there were two unsuccessful attempts, initiated respectively by Duvergier de Hauranne and Rémusat, to promote parliamentary reforms that would have extended the franchise and admitted a broader spectrum of the middle class into the electorate. Following the failure of these initiatives the Banquet campaign emerged as a direct attempt to take the debate to the country, intended to raise support among the lower middle classes whose disillusion with the regime was growing. Banquets were held from July 1847, with many of the speakers taking up the issue of corruption, and in some of the provincial banquets demands for social reforms were also voiced. These early banquets were extremely moderate in their tone, but after the Lille banquet in November 1847 the movement was increasingly radicalised, especially as republicans became involved. It was at this point that the government showed its concern, and the King's Speech in December 1847 denounced the volatile language of the Banqueteers (**71**). Supporters of the government in the Chamber now felt obliged to adopt a firm line, and a further attempt to widen the franchise was defeated on 12 February. This failure undoubtedly had a polarising effect. The reformers realised that the chances of change coming from the existing Chamber were remote and so the radicals resolved to hold a banquet of protest on 22 February. The moderate reformers under the leadership of Barrot and Thiers were now losing control of the campaign which had been motivated to reform the electoral system and depose Guizot*. Now, more radical politicians were challenging the whole basis of the regime.

The government was becoming alarmed and therefore banned the banquet. Nevertheless, demonstrators began to gather in the city on the afternoon of 22 February. On 23 February the King resolved to dismiss Guizot and replace him with Molé. It was too late, and that evening soldiers fired on a crowd of demonstrators who were protesting at the banning of the banquet. By the following morning some 1500 barricades had been erected throughout the city. But the situation was still only one of protest that had turned into riot. It is the advantage of hindsight that tempts the historian to impose a pattern on events. What caused this situation to slip beyond the government's retrieval? There were two immediate factors, both of which relate to the failure of the regime itself. In the first instance, the defection of several units of the National Guard, who handed over their weapons to the rioters, meant that the government was unable to organise an effective repression. Secondly, there was the collective *malaise* that consumed both the King and upper-middle-class supporters of the regime. There was in effect a dual abdication: Louis Philippe abdicated his throne and the *grande bourgeoisie* abdicated responsibility (**71**). The power vacuum that resulted from this collective paralysis enabled political activists in the republican camp to steal the initiative and mobilise mass support in the capital (**38**). The invasion of the Chamber on 24 February by armed insurgents (who had presumably acquired weapons from the defecting National Guardsmen) was a decisive event, since it dispossessed the elite politicians of all confidence. Mere protest was receding and accumulated social and political discontents were being politicised in a manner which now   med a revolutionary intent. Moreover, 'Orleanism was pragmat. rather than a true system of principles and convictions, and as such could hardly arouse any fanatical defenders' (**60**). Yet while it had been political factors, particularly the breakdown of prevailing political loyalties within the middle classes, which initially prompted protest, it should not be forgotten that social discontents provided the emotional adrenalin of those who built the barricades. Pent-up social dissatisfactions now exploded in the city: Louis Philippe's château at Neuilly was looted; in Lyon, silk workers attacked monasteries; and there was a major strike at Limoges. In the countryside there were assaults on tax officers and carters attacked railway yards (**60**).

De Tocqueville*, in his famous *Recollections*, described how, on 24 February, he returned home after Louis Philippe's abdication to find his brother and sister-in-law waiting in his house. He recalled that his sister-in-law had lost her head: 'She already saw her husband dead and her daughters raped' (**7**). De Tocqueville promptly arranged for his sister-in-law to leave Paris for the safety of the countryside. Such happenings were probably not uncommon among the *grands bourgeois* families of Paris, and Marx and Engels had certainly hit the right note in their *Communist Manifesto*, first published in February 1848, when they crowed: 'Let the ruling classes tremble at a Communistic revolution' (**3**). But the fear and anticipation of the respectable classes were probably greater than events warranted. The February Revolution was a relatively bloodless affair, with only those who took to the streets risking death. The new Provisional Government was made up of moderate men, and even the socialist Louis Blanc* would be condemned by later generations of revolutionary socialists as having been unprepared and too soft. Nevertheless, bourgeois fear of what the revolution represented was decisive in determining the subsequent history of the French Second Republic. In particular it explains the steady movement to the right that resulted eventually in the election of Louis Napoléon as the Republic's first (and only) President.

The policies pursued by the new Provisional Government were essentially moderate. The leading member of the government, Lamartine, was no Robespierre, and he sought moderate solutions. He was by nature a cautious man and he had no grand designs or great schemes like Louis Blanc*. Nor did he possess the grasp of political and administrative detail that was the gift of Ledru-Rollin, the Minister of the Interior. Lamartine took on responsibility for the conduct of foreign affairs, matters which consumed much of the Provisional Government's time. This may seem surprising, since it had been acute social and economic disorders that had brought people onto the streets of Paris. As far as Lamartine was concerned, however, the unemployed would have to trust in Louis Blanc*. In the meantime, his priority was to allay the fears of the other European powers. He did this by publishing a *Manifesto to Europe*, issued within two weeks of Louis Philippe's abdication. 'Half a century,' Lamartine wrote, 'separates 1792 from 1848. To return after the lapse of half a century to the principle of 1792, or to the principle of conquest pursued during the Empire, would not be to advance but to retrogress. . . . The world and ourselves are desirous of advancing fraternity and peace' (2). It was a sensible move, as it forestalled the possibility of foreign intervention, but it also indicated that the government was not primarily concerned with the social discontents which had brought the Paris workers onto the streets.

Once the threat of foreign intervention had been removed, it was possible for the Provisional Government to attend to other matters – namely finance, political consolidation of the regime, and the social question. In all three areas the government was found lacking, although, to be fair, the difficulty of consolidating the regime in face of the political and social conservatism of rural France was extreme. In addition, the solutions sought by the government often only created more of the same type of problems or exacerbated existing ones. This was certainly the case in financial matters. It had been a financial disaster that had caused Louis Philippe's government to forfeit bourgeois support, but the Provisional Government did not succeed in restoring bourgeois confidence in the weeks and months immediately after February 1848. Uncertainty continued to prevail in the business world and was reflected by a dramatic decline in the normally stable share index of the Bank of France. There was also a considerable decline in gold reserves – from 226 million francs in February to 59 million francs by mid-March (79). The combined effect of the fall in the Bank of France's share index and the shrinkage of gold reserves was to restrict lending by commercial and provincial banks, resulting in a general strangulation of credit facilities. This was to have serious social consequences. In the short run, however, a decline in the fortunes of the country's national bank meant a decline in the financial stability of the government itself. In fact the government's deficit rose rapidly during March and consequently a 45-centime tax on direct income was introduced. This tax fell predominantly on the landed classes and its effects were most severely felt by the smaller farmers and peasant proprietors. In the later elections for the Constituent Assembly, rural France squarely rejected republicanism. Whether this was due exclusively to the 45-centime tax or to clerical influence does not matter. The effect of the tax was undoubtedly to make the consolidation of the republican regime more difficult. In the Department of the Lot, for instance, it was necessary for the authorities to call in troops on no less than nine occasions in order to secure the collection of the hated tax (**18, 97**).

On the question of political consolidation the Provisional Government was no more successful. As Minister of the Interior, Ledru-Rollin was responsible for the organisation of the elections for the Constituent Assembly which, the republicans hoped, would draw up a comprehensive republican constitution and so validate the revolution of February. On 2 March the Provisional Government introduced universal suffrage, thus enfranchising nine million new voters. The idealism of the republicans led them to believe that universal suffrage would deliver France into a new age of equality and social progress. The cynical observed that France had been delivered into the hands of the fickle peasantry. More correctly, it might be said that the fate of France now rested with the Church, for although the clergy welcomed the demise of Louis Philippe they were less than pleased with ensuing demands from socialists and radical republicans for an end to Church control of primary education (**91**). It was hardly surprising, then, that the clerical opposition to republicanism in the Constituent Assembly elections of April was nothing less than implacable. The bishops drew up lists of acceptable candidates which the priests recommended to their parishioners [**doc. 5**]. For their part, the republicans, particularly those to the left, argued for a delay in the holding of the elections to provide an opportunity for educating the electorate along republican lines. Ledru-Rollin also did his best to carry out an administrative purge by dismissing monarchist prefects and replacing them with republicans (**90**). The elections were therefore a struggle between republican bureaucracy and clerical influence, and the outcome showed that clericalism was a far more durable and entrenched tradition than republicanism (**65**).

The elections were held on Easter Sunday 1848. Leaving aside the weight of clerical pressure, it is hardly surprising that a politically inexperienced electorate should have expressed a preference for familiar local notables. There was also intense provincial hostility to anything that emanated from Paris, a hostility which extended to republicanism. Thus the result of the elections, although disappointing to the republicans, was not altogether surprising. Over half the deputies elected were on the right: 200 Orleanists, 150 legitimists and a further 350 committed to the clerical campaign for freedom of education. Of the remainder, about 250 were for the most part moderate republicans. There was only a small minority of seventy to eighty radical and socialist republicans. A further indication of the social composition of the Assembly was that some 700 of the 900 deputies paid tax in excess of 500 francs per annum (**53**). There were also a considerable number of educated and professional men – 176 lawyers and 170 public officials (**38**). The political centre of gravity of the Constituent Assembly, then, was certainly weighted towards the interests of property, and although deputies might label themselves 'moderate republican', this did not necessarily indicate the nature of their political attitudes or intentions.

An Assembly so comprehensively dominated by men of property was unlikely to be radical in dealing with the other great priority facing the Second Republic: the social problem. Moreover, the conservative elements of society were beginning to recover from the initial shock of the February upheaval, and a conservative majority in the Assembly no doubt increased bourgeois confidence. The essence of the social problem in the capital was unemployment, which was still quite high in the spring of 1848. Moreover, this situation had also contributed to the fact that radical groups had stolen the political initiative in Paris at the end of February. Thus the conservatives in the Assembly needed to disarm the radicals if more moderate forces were to gain ascendancy in government and society once again. Yet any hopes of wide-ranging public works were dashed when the Assembly insisted that the Provisional Government should be replaced by a new five-man Executive Commission of which Louis Blanc* was not a member. There was also considerable opposition to the National Workshops Scheme*, and the leading spokesman of the right on this question, the Comte de Falloux, claimed that the Workshops provided the potential for future revolutionary outbreaks. Consequently the demand by the radicals and the socialists for programmes of public works to alleviate unemployment went unheeded. Further, moderate republicans like Lamartine also were suspicious of a radical demand to liberate Poland. On 15 May a crowd of workers led by politicians from the radical clubs gathered outside the Assembly building. Eventually the crowd surged into the main body of the hall and broke up the meeting, and one of the club leaders, Aloysius Huber, proclaimed a new Provisional Government. If this was a planned uprising, with the radicals hoping that the Paris workers would follow their lead, then it was a vain hope. Nevertheless, it did give the government the excuse to arrest a number of radical leaders and it was now demonstrably clear that the radicals were becoming more and more isolated. The counter-revolution had already begun, for in the previous month fifty-nine workers had been killed by troops in Rouen after a protest about the failure of radicals in the elections (**79**).

Contemporary opinion saw society becoming increasingly divided, and it was in these circumstances that on 28 May [**docs 6a–b**] the Club de la Montagne de Montmartre called for a people's banquet in direct imitation of the bourgeois banquets which had been held in 1847. The Assembly detected in such an event a likelihood of disorder, and its organisers were promptly arrested (**86**). In the following month the Assembly announced its intention to ditch the scheme of National Workshops*. The rumours of a workers' insurrection which had permeated the police reports of the previous weeks [**doc. 6b**] were now confirmed. Barricades were erected, but Cavaignac's troops, acting for the government, were ruthless in their suppression of the uprising. Initially the revolutionaries lost some 400 to 500 men, but those who fled were flushed out from the narrow alleyways of Paris and some 3000 were cut down. The Russian exile Alexander Herzen, who witnessed the event, observed that Russian Cossack troops were as meek as lambs compared with the barbarous French soldiers (**12**). A further 11,693 people were charged in connection with these events and many of them were deported to Algeria (**40**).

The 'June Days' uprising was a remarkable event in the history of the Second Republic. The initial responses of contemporaries, particularly Marx and de Tocqueville* [**docs 7a, b**], emphasised the divided nature of French society, with the uprising interpreted primarily as a struggle between those who had a stake in society and those who did not. Modern historical investigation has disputed the simplicity of contemporary analysis, and the work of Gossez (**97**), in particular, has shown that the uprising was not a straightforward conflict between rich and poor as de Tocqueville suggested [**doc. 7b**] or between *bourgeoisie* and proletariat as Marx believed [**doc. 7a**]. In fact, those who were involved in the repression were not only middle-class types – property-owners, shopkeepers, clerks and professionals – but also young workers who had volunteered for the National Guard, either because they needed employment (**84**) or perhaps because they had not been fully assimilated into the craft communities (**38**). The class lines of the conflict are certainly difficult for the modern historian to discern. One thing is clear though: middle-class prejudice over alleged working-class brutality and depravity (**64**) was a potent force, and probably helps to explain why many middle- and lower-middle-class Parisians were prepared to support the repression. They feared that otherwise working-class barbarism might have the effect of cancelling out the gains of the revolution of February.

The debate on the June Days uprising was not settled by the findings of Gossez, although there is general agreement that there were representatives of all classes and all sorts and conditions of men on both sides of the conflict. An examination by a left-wing historian, George Rudé, of the occupations of those who were arrested has not supported the conclusions of Marx and de Tocqueville*. Rudé's examination reveals that the insurgents came from similar occupations to those who had been involved in the storming of the Bastille in 1789. There were 554 stonemasons, 510 joiners, 283 painters, 140 carpenters, along with a large number of cabinet-makers, locksmiths and jewellers. Rudé further contends that independent craftsmen outnumbered wage earners – or, to use Marxist terminology, new proletarians – by about two to one. From this he concludes that the June Days was not strictly a modern class conflict, a polarisation between *bourgeoisie* and proletariat. Rather, it was a more traditional form of protest by older independent crafts and small producers. Nevertheless, he does accept that transport workers and *mécaniciens* (engineering workers), part of the newer wage-earning proletariat, provided the militant hard core of the insurgents, although he doubts that the Parisian proletariat was fully formed (**40**). The majority of Parisian workers, especially in the craft occupations, still operated independently or in small workshops of fewer than ten people (**79**).

The work of Gossez and Rudé undoubtedly provided an important corrective to initial conclusions about the rising. However, more recent examinations of the participants have produced conclusions that are clearly aligned with those of Marx (**80**). Using sophisticated statistical techniques, Tilly and Lees have found that proletarians figured disproportionately among those who were arrested. Although they agree that building workers (stonemasons, carpenters and joiners) were conspicuous in their participation, they emphasise that other groups – metal-workers, leather-workers, transport workers and, to a lesser extent, printing workers and those involved in chemicals – figure to an extent that reasserts the validity of Marx's original analysis [**doc. 7c**]. They also stress that the insurgents came disproportionately from those workers employed in the larger firms and workshops. Further, the building, metals and leather trades had quite a well-established tradition of organisation and co-operation. It would seem then, that Marx's contention has a degree of

61

statistical substantiation that Gossez and Rudé overlooked. At the
same time, de Tocqueville's* assertion that the June Days was a
struggle between rich and poor [**doc. 7b**] may also have some
validity, because the majority of those arrested came from the
central and south-eastern *arrondissements* of the city which were also
the poorest measured by tax returns (**80**).

There are other considerations to take into account. What, for
instance, was the role of the migrant worker in the events of June?
Most of those arrested were immigrants from other parts of France,
particularly from the north-east (**64, 79, 80**) where they may have
already experienced the industrial way of life. Rural Frenchmen,
except those from departments immediately contiguous to Paris,
were apparently less likely to move to the capital, although there
were rural workers employed seasonally in the construction industry
(**75**). Those, on the other hand, who gave their support to the army
were very often peasant volunteers who had come from outside
Paris, together with shopkeepers, merchants and landlords (**80**). It
should not be thought that peasant immigrants were always on the
side of reaction, although this may have been generally so in the
case of those who came to Paris. Elsewhere, for instance in Marseille, the more recently arrived often supplied the groups of
politically active democrats, republicans and socialists. The artisans
of Marseille had been traditionally clericalist and royalist in their
allegiance, but this ceased to be so from the 1840s, and this political
shift has largely been attributed to the influx of *étrangers* (or immigrants), many of whom were peasants (**107**). Political allegiances,
then, were often determined by peculiar local conditions. If the debate on the June Days has demonstrated one thing, it is that there
was no straight-line relationship between class and political behaviour.

In the countryside the pattern is no clearer. It is often assumed
that the peasantry gravitated to the political right. Peasant voting
patterns for the Constituent Assembly go some way towards con-
firming such a conclusion. At the same time, provincial notables
became even more determined after the June Days to put their
political weight behind conservatism. However, the June Days also
focused the political imagination of republican radicals who
recognised the precarious nature of a revolution that was centred
exclusively in the capital. Thus throughout the autumn of 1848, the
activity of the left-wing republican pressure group, *Solidarité
Républicaine*, was directed towards the promotion of democratic and
socialist values among the peasants. This paid off in the elections of
May 1849 which produced a political polarisation. Admittedly,

right-wing candidates made considerable progress, but at the same time the extreme left made incursions, primarily at the expense of the moderate republican vote. The growth of peasant republicanism, and with it a potential socialism, had already manifested itself in some parts of the south: in the presidential elections of December 1848, the left-wing candidates, Ledru-Rollin and Raspail, commanded slightly more than 20 per cent of the poll. In 1850 the people of the Var voted three to one for left-wing candidates (**61**). Thus, outside the industrial north-east, support for the left was strongest in the rural areas of the south and south-east, principally the Var and Bouches du Rhône (**60, 71, 83**). Elsewhere, the peasant vote, in the north and west for example, was drawn to the right. Louis Napoléon's support was strongest in the northern departments of Somme, Oise and Aisne and in the western areas of Charente, Vienne and Deux-Sèvres. Peasant politics cannot be explained, then, purely in terms of deference and allegiance to local notables. Just as the politics of the towns were framed by a complex mesh of influences, so too were the politics of the countryside. Peasants were often concerned with the defence of their ancient rights, and there had already been peasant campaigns against the Forest Codes of 1827 and 1837 in the Pyrenees, in the Alpine areas and in the Massif Central (**79**). At the same time rural artisans were also to be found moving to the political left (**61**).

There is, then, a sense in which concentration on the June Days is perhaps misleading, as it does not necessarily reveal the true nature of social-political divisions in France. Most Frenchmen still lived in small towns that were economically dependent on the land. Even Paris was subject to sharp fluctuations in the prices of agricultural produce, as has already been indicated. This was because most towns, Paris included, were economically governed by their immediate hinterlands, since the transport system, both road and rail, was so weakly developed in the 1840s (**78**). The Paris Basin and northern France were essentially grain-growing areas and it was a crisis in grain that was the central feature of 1846 and 1847 (**55, 94**). In that sense, then, the social crisis that consumed Paris in the winter and spring of 1848 was more of a pre-industrial crisis than the kind suggested by Marx. Nevertheless, the concentration of political power in Paris makes it natural that historians have regarded events in the capital as of primary importance.

The political consequence of the June Days was a growing strength of the right. Louis Napoléon's appeal was essentially populist, and he received support from all social groups – the notables, middle classes, the workers and peasants. The myth of Bonapartism was powerful among the peasantry, and politicians like Molé* and Thiers believed that Louis Napoléon could be controlled and that his popularity could be used to defend the fabric of society. The name of Bonaparte was intimately connected with order, which was what most Frenchmen sought after June. It was also the name associated with national glory, and the lack-lustre performance of France during the Orleanist years may have drawn men to the Bonapartist cause. Many of the older peasants would have remembered the Empire as a period of prosperity as well as glory, and may have compared it wistfully with their current misfortunes – depression in agriculture and the 45-centime tax. Thus peasant support for Louis Napoléon may been partly a protest against republican taxation policy. At the same time some middle-class voters may have been attracted to Louis Napoléon because of his statements in favour of a measure of religious control over education. But for the most part support stemmed from negative calculations: a vote for Louis Napoléon by the working class was a vote against Cavaignac, the 'butcher of June'. In the same way, at the opposite end of the social spectrum, many legitimist notables were attracted to Louis Napoléon because businessmen were attracted to Cavaignac (**79, 84**). The presidential elections of December were also a vote for order. Louis Napoléon polled well over five million votes and Cavaignac over a million. Their nearest rival was Ledru-Rollin, with a mere 370,119 votes. Both Louis Napoléon and Cavaignac were men of order. The latter had already demonstrated his commitment by the repression of June, whilst the former traded on the Bonapartist legend to suggest that he too was a champion of order.

Once Louis Napoléon had been elected President, the Constituent Assembly voted for its own dissolution, in January 1849. Louis Napoléon's first cabinet was dominated by legitimists, Orleanists and members of the Dynastic Opposition*, including Barrot. Louis Napoléon was now in a position to consolidate his hold over French government and society. He resorted to traditional methods of administrative manipulation, and purged the prefecture of its republican personnel. Despite his precautions, the left was still able to establish a presence in the elections for the legislature held in May 1849, and this reflected the growing appeal of the *Solidarité Républicaine*. There were some seventy-five to eighty moderate republicans in the new chamber and 180 radical and socialist republicans. Conservative deputies were still in the majority, winning about 500 seats, 200 being won by legitimists. The conservative representation was comprised mainly of notables and wealthy magnates. They viewed the continued presence of left-wing republicans – known as *Montagnards** – with alarm. The apparent danger of the left may have been magnified by its geographical concentration (see above). In fact, however, the left was still weak, as was shown when it orchestrated an attempt at insurrection on 13 June 1849 in protest at French troops being sent to Rome to restore the papacy (see below, pp. 96–7). The insurrection was a failure, and its only effect was to reinforce the resolve of the conservatives to carry out political repression. By the following year the conservatives were in the ascendancy, and in May the Legislative Assembly disenfranchised all those who had criminal records, and all those who did not fulfil a three-year residential qualification. It was an action directed against what Thiers called the 'vile multitude', and of course it greatly reduced the support of the left republicans.

If Molé* and Thiers believed that they could continue manipulating Louis Napoléon at will, they were soon to be disillusioned. The movement towards dictatorship was quickening. Bonapartism had gained considerable support in the Chamber, and Louis Napoléon kept up a vigorous propaganda campaign through a number of provincial tours. Repression too was growing: steps had been taken against 185 newspapers by December 1850 (**75**). Eventually, in December 1851, a carefully planned coup effectively overthrew the Republic. There was resistance – workers in Paris put up barricades – but it was easily crushed. In the provinces there were pockets of resistance, and much of this peasant activity formed the germ of later peasant socialism (**75, 102**). Peasants attacked the houses of money-lenders and tax collectors, destroying papers and account books. In the village of Taigny the people attacked the church and smashed the confessionals, claiming that they had been used by the priests as places in which to fornicate secretly with women of the village (**79**). Such was the elemental nature of peasant discontent. Stemming from frustration with economic privation and uncertainty, peasant action was uncoordinated. The Second Republic had come to an end.

8 The Habsburg Lands

If there are such things as turning points in history, then nine o'clock in the evening of 13 March 1848 must surely qualify for that status in the history of the Habsburg Empire. It was then that Metternich, the Austrian Chancellor, tendered his resignation to the Emperor Ferdinand. Metternich was the symbol of the old order and his name was synonymous with the Settlement of 1815. His fall was the result of the coincidence of two historical trends. On the one hand, his resignation was a response to the clamour for liberal reform which had reached a crescendo with the news of the revolution in Paris. The Habsburg Court needed to sacrifice someone if it was to have any credence with the nationalities, particularly the Magyars. On the other hand, Metternich's depature was also a response to a conspiracy within the Imperial Court itself. He had simply been in power too long, and those who felt blocked from power, principally Kolowrat*, were only too pleased to see the seventy-four-year-old Chancellor relinquish office.

For some historians this lack of cohesion within the ruling elite has been regarded as a more pertinent source of breakdown than a general dislocation of society ensuing from rapid economic and social change (**53**). Viewed from this standpoint, Metternich's resignation is not part of the history of the revolution; rather it is an episode in the internal political manoeuvres of a closed system. There is no doubt that Metternich's ability to handle affairs with singleness of purpose had been steadily impaired from 1835 onwards. From that date he had to administer the Empire in consultation with the newly appointed Regent, Archduke Ludwig, and the ambitious Kolowrat*. Perhaps, then, there is a case for suggesting that the collapse of the government in Vienna was as much the result of the failure of individuals as it was the product of social unrest and demands for political reform. In fact, the revolution in the Habsburg lands really needs to be appreciated from three standpoints. There was a middle-class liberal revolution that demanded constitutional reform and responsible government; there was a national revolution; and there was also a social, primarily agrarian, revolution. (**147**)

Nevertheless, Metternich's resignation and his hasty departure to the town of Feldsberg, 64 kilometres outside Vienna, followed by his flight across revolutionary Europe to London, represented a major victory for the revolution. It was a conscious break with the past, and the Habsburgs were pushed along the path of liberalism, albeit for a short distance. The meeting of the *Diet* of Lower Austria had occasioned demands for administrative reforms, the abolition of censorship and ultimately a constitution. By April a constitution had been granted for the German part of the Empire together with Bohemia, Moravia and Galicia. At this stage it appeared that the radical elements – mainly students – were achieving their aims, and by 17 May the Imperial Court had fled to Innsbruck. The flight of the Court was a further indication of the profound shock and loss of confidence being experienced by the dynasty. This certainly seems to be a feature of the revolutions in central Europe, most noticeably in Prussia, whereas in France by May 1848 the leading bourgeois politicians were already planning to suppress the original revolutionary fervour.

How was it that the most powerful of the European despotisms collapsed in the face of a few riots and the call for reform from the *Diet*? How was it that Metternich, the most resolute defender of order and loyal supporter of the dynasty, was discarded so readily by the Habsburg Court? Of course the regime was shocked by the enormity and scale of the outbreaks throughout its domains, but this alone is not a satisfactory explanation of the dynasty's rapid capitulation. Answers to these questions can be found by examining the growing problems that the Habsburgs were facing from 1835 until the revolution of March 1848. This so-called *Vormarz* period dates from the death of Francis I and has sometimes been called the era of 'despotism without a despot', for Francis' successor, Ferdinand, was unfortunately a feeble-minded idiot. The Court resolved to establish a *Staatskonferenz*, which was nominally under the chairmanship of Ferdinand but was actually managed by the Archduke Ludwig. The other members of the *Konferenz* were Metternich, Kolowrat* and the Archduke Karl. From this time onwards the effectiveness of Metternich's control was diluted and the regime was gripped with immobility, 'not the purposeful immobility imposed by a single will, but the stalemate that results from equal and opposite forces' (**148**). This stemmed from the rivalry between Metternich and Kolowrat, and it was this conflict that allowed the regime to 'drift into a state of inertia that made any real accomplishments impossible' (**152**). Programmes of reform were outlined by civil servants, such as Francis Stadion*, but no action was taken (**148**).

The durability of the regime was also affected in other ways. State finances were in a parlous state and steps were taken to limit the size of the army; the Empire's international trading position was deteriorating in face of growing competition from the *Zollverein* states; and in foreign affairs Metternich seemed no longer able to guarantee the co-operation of other states in the suppression of revolutionary activity. Austria had become estranged from Russia after Metternich's failure to secure a diplomatic marriage between Stephen, the son of the Palatine of Hungary, and the Tsar's daughter, Olga. On the home front the Empire seemed unable to grapple with the consequences of economic and social change which were particularly acute in the countryside. The material conditions of the peasantry had undoubtedly been worsening throughout the *Vormarz* period, especially in Bohemia, northern Hungary, Silesia, Galicia and Transylvania (see above, Chapter 4). This was not just a matter of dealing with peasant protest against the performance of the feudal labour rent, the *Robot**, but also a question of meeting the demands of those rural landlords who were increasingly being drawn into market operations. This was especially the case in the Hungarian lands, where Magyar landlords recognised the inefficiency of the *Robot* system and sought its abolition. The Hungarian economic writer Stephen Szechenyi* reckoned that a free man's labour was three times more productive than that of a peasant performing the *Robot* as labour rent. Yet such cost-effective claims were lost on the Habsburg state.

The most pressing problem that the Habsburgs faced in the *Vormarz* period was the rising tide of nationalism, not only from the Magyars and Italians, who were to grab centre-stage in 1848, but also from the Poles, Romanians, Czechs, Croatians, Slovaks and Slovenes. The Habsburg response to the nationality question seems to have been altogether clumsy. This is amply demonstrated in two episodes: the first was the occupation of the free city of Cracow in February 1846 and the subsequent Austrian annexation in November of that year. The Austrian action was intended to be pre-emptive and designed to quell the possibility of an uprising among the Polish subjects of the Empire, but its effect was to isolate Austria internationally. The city of Cracow had been independent since the Settlement of 1815 and the Habsburg action was condemned by Britain and by the smaller German states. Condemnation by Britain was probably bearable, but the loss of support from the small German states weakened Austria in the politics of the *Bund* and depressed Austria's status relative to Prussia. Thus Austria's 'moral credit was weakened everywhere' (**148**). Moreover, the annexation of Cracow only exacerbated the nationality problem, as it fuelled a growing resentment among the Poles of Habsburg Galicia. The second episode that undermined Austria's international standing and revealed the clumsiness of the Empire was Radetzky's* unilateral decision to occupy Ferrara in the Papal States in July 1847. Again the motive would seem to have been precautionary: the papal reforms had excited liberal hopes throughout the Papal States and also in the Habsburg provinces of Lombardy and Venetia, and Radetzky thought that a show of force would stem the appetite for reform. As such his move was counter-productive, and it meant that Austria's claim to be the defender of the existing order had now lost all legitimacy (**169, 172**).

The national oppositions grew steadily throughout the *Vormarz* period, but the regime could probably have withstood such discontent if it had not been for the growth of a middle-class liberal opposition in Vienna itself. This opposition made itself felt in the *Diet* of Lower Austria where the more liberal elements of the lesser nobility began to form links with the middle-class intelligentsia. Middle-class opinion was broadly articulated through such organisations as the Legal-Political Reading Club, the Concordia Society and the Lower Austrian Manufacturers' Association. Writers such as Franz Schuselka had attacked the political privileges of the Church, while Karl Beidtel sought financial and fiscal reforms. Thus when the news of the Paris revolution reached Vienna there was already a proto-liberal opposition in existence. Further, this opposition gained in confidence when the contents of Kossuth's speech at the *Diet* of Pressburg* became known. The speech was translated into German by a Hungarian journalist living in Vienna and quickly distributed by the Legal-Political Reading Club. The middle-class opposition now called itself the 'party of progress' and advocated the creation of a responsible government, a broader franchise, reform of the civil service, abolition of censorship, religious toleration, universal education and the formation of a citizens' militia. It is important to recognise that this opposition, under the leadership of Bach* and Lohner, was loyal to the dynasty. It merely wished to reform the system of government and get rid of Metternich (**152**). The opposition programme quickly attracted support from all quarters, including the *Diet* and also the students who were active in mobilising the workers.

The rapidity of the revolution's success was remarkable, as the Court quickly assented to the demands of the reformers. On 14 March the Court accepted the idea of setting up a civic guard; censorship was lifted; and the Emperor agreed to the formulation of some kind of constitution. But this latter concession, on the face of it the most important, was in fact rather limited. Thus, although Metternich had been vanquished, the achievements of the revolution in Vienna should not be overemphasised. Significantly, the new government contained representatives of the old order, including Kolowrat* and Ficquelmont*.

Outside the capital events were taking a more dramatic turn, especially in Hungary. After Kossuth's speech in Pressburg*, and the demonstrations in Budapest which followed it, a liberal government was formed under the premiership of Lajos Batthyany. Apparently, some 20,000 demonstrators had taken to the streets in Budapest but the garrison, made up largely of Italian conscripts, was not used as it was thought to be unreliable (**145**). The other members of the Hungarian cabinet were Kossuth, Szechenyi*, Deak and Eotvos. The new Hungarian government espoused both national and liberal sentiments, as expressed in the 'March Laws' which abolished the *Robot** and made provision for the election of a parliament on a restricted property franchise. Knowledge of the Magyar language was to be an essential qualification for any intending candidate in an election [**doc. 2d**]. This meant that the Magyars would effectively dominate the Slavic minorities in the eastern part of the Empire: at the same time they would establish an ascendancy over a substantial number of Romanians. The whole design of the March Laws would seem to have been an attempt by the Magyar nobility and lesser gentry to substitute themselves for the German-Austrian ruling class. They certainly aimed to save the lower nobles from economic decline and 'consequent political extinction' (**145**). Whether the Magyars' political ambition was so consciously calculated has been questioned, and it may be that they just did not understand the ambitions of the Croatians and Romanians. In this context their programme was less one of 'conscious aggression . . . than of naive optimism' (**148**). Significantly, although there were some Magyars who were not landowners, there were no non-Magyars who owned any sizeable holdings (**42**). However, the March Laws were economically progressive and owed much to the ideas of Szechenyi*.

Magyar ambition was also the source of its defeat; for the Hungarian revolution aroused the latent racial antagonisms that existed between the Magyars and Slavic minorities. This was well recognised by Kolowrat* when he appointed Joseph Jellacic as governor of Croatia on 22 March 1848. Jellacic was ardently anti-Magyar and he was eventually a prime mover in the suppression of the Magyar revolution.

Events in Vienna were now moving rapidly. The Crown had already agreed in April to a constitution which included elected assemblies that would share legislative power with the Emperor. But by the summer the students and middle-class intellectuals were beginning to articulate a much more assertive policy, and had found in Dr Adolf Fischhof a dynamic spokesman who headed a revolutionary committee. It was at this point that the Court fled to Innsbruck. The revolutionary committee demanded a new ministry and forced the resignation of Pillersdorf, as well as the election of a Constituent Assembly which duly met in mid-July. Its most outstanding achievement was the abolition of the *Robot** – an achievement which was not reversed even during the counter-revolutionary era of neo-absolutism after the abdication of Ferdinand and the crowning of Franz-Josef. But this achievement also heralded the break-up of the revolutionary forces, for the peasants, who had been facing an acute agrarian crisis since 1845, now became detached from the revolution.

Elsewhere the forces of nationalism were still at work. If Magyar nationalism was sufficiently virile to seek to subdue other minorities, this was not the case with Czech nationalism, which was the mainspring of the revolution in Prague, in the northern part of the Empire. Like the patriotic movement in Italy, the national movement among the Czechs was largely the preserve of an urban intelligentsia. Its leading exponent was Frantisek Palacky, the Czech historian (see above, p. 38). Bohemia, where the majority of the Czechs lived, was a region of developing industry where the entrepreneurial classes were largely of German-Jewish origin, and in almost all respects the Czechs were in the 'hands of the Germans' (**151**). Germans dominated the bureaucracy, the clergy, business and land.

Czech nationalism had its roots, then, in the history of foreign domination. The Czech movement in 1848 had made its first move on 11 March when a meeting of intellectuals took place at the Wenzelsbad inn* and proclaimed a liberal programme – freedom of the press and abolition of the *Robot**. The Czech movement was nonetheless limited, if not realistic in its ambition, as even at this early stage the Wenzelsbad Programme expressed a desire to maintain a 'constitutional link between the lands of the Bohemian Crown' and the monarchy. The monarchy was petitioned and demands for a constitution and for the recognition of the Czech language in education and administration were accepted.

Czech nationalism was only one strand in a more broadly based Slavic movement, which reached its climax in June 1848 when a Pan-Slav Congress was convened in Prague under the chairmanship of Palacky. The earlier Wenzelsbad Programme* now became the basis of Austro-Slavism – the demand that the various Slavic minorities, including the Czechs, should be given a degree of autonomy within the Habsburg Empire. Palacky took the view that had the Austrian Empire not existed then it would have been necessary to invent it in order to protect the Slavic minorities from a predatory Russia [**doc. 2c**]. His programme, however, was not likely to be accepted either by the monarchy or by those Germans who lived in Bohemia – according to Engels there were seventeen Germans to every twenty-four Czechs living in the region. More to the point, the Germans formed the core of the urban middle class, while the Czech and other Slavic peoples were largely confined to proletarian and peasant occupations. The indications of German dominance were already far too great to allow any form of true Slavic independence. A. J. P. Taylor has criticised Austro-Slavism, saying that it was 'a programme of timidity' and that 'the dynasty was asked to give the Slav peoples the freedom that they were too weak to take for themselves' (**88**). This rather harsh comment ignores the reality of power within the monarchy. Perhaps the view that Austro-Slavism intended to promote a moderate federalist solution along historical-political lines is more just (**146**). It can be argued that the Slav Congress and the Federalist programme showed the first resistance of Slavic peoples to German or Magyar domination (**160**).

Whatever conclusion is drawn about the significance of Palacky's programme, the Slav Congress occasioned the first decisive step in carrying out the counter-revolution. A student rising in Prague which overlapped with worker unrest in the city's cotton mills gave the Imperial Governor of Moravia, Windischgratz, the excuse to bombard the city. The unrest had been growing for some time and stemmed from increasing unemployment in the face of technological innovation. This problem was aggravated by a famine of cotton supplies from America, which could no longer be brought through the port of Trieste since the Habsburgs were blockading it as part of their military campaign against the Italians (**148**). The relatively easy suppression of the Czech revolution and the subsequent victory over the Italians at Custozza did much to revive Habsburg confidence.

Although the Habsburgs were starting a counter-revolution against the Italians and the Czechs, the monarchy was still prepared to make concessions to the Hungarians. In all essentials the Habsburgs were at first prepared to countenance the March Laws (see above, p. 70 and **doc. 2d**). Thus on 2 July the Palatine of Hungary, Archduke Stephen, opened the new Hungarian parliament, which subsequently passed legislation to establish a separate Hungarian army and an independent Hungarian budget. This was virtually complete autonomy and the Habsburgs were now able to capitalise on the latent hostility of the Croatians, Serbs and Romanians towards Magyar nationalism. The monarchy, now recovering under the ambitious personality of the Archduchess Sophie*, sent Jellacic, an ardent Croatian, to suppress the revolution. In September his troops entered Hungary. The liberal Count Batthyany resigned and power passed into the hands of the radical, Kossuth, who became a virtual dictator (**149**). The other liberal members of the cabinet had also given way – Szechenyi* attempted suicide and was committed to an asylum; Esterhazy resigned; and Eotvos fled to Germany. All of Kossuth's energy was now poured into raising an army to block Jellacic's advance.

At this point it is important to understand how the various revolutionary movements became intertwined: news of plans to send part of the Viennese garrison to assist Jellacic was widely rumoured in Vienna. It was this rumour that signalled a demonstration of protest by the student members of the Academic Legion and the workers. Although there was a small element of mutiny in the garrison, the October Days uprising, as it became known, really marked the end of the Vienna revolution. The lynching of Count Latour, one of the members of the cabinet, frightened the Imperial family, who fled to Olmutz, a small town in Moravia. The October Days was the most startling of revolutionary events since it highlighted the polarised situation between the classes. Not only did it herald the departure of the Court; it also frightened moderate liberal politicians who sought to escape from Vienna. The number of refugees has been estimated at 100,000 and practically 'all members of the bourgeoisie left the city' (**148**). Windischgratz now prepared to regain control of the capital. He was given plenipotentiary powers to take whatever actions he thought appropriate. He besieged the city and began a steady bombardment which killed between 3000 and 5000 people (**26**). The October Days were Vienna's equivalent of Paris's June Days. Both indicated a divergence of ideals and expectations and both marked a defeat for the revolution. In Vienna the suppression of the October Days was a real turning-point, since the Viennese *bourgeoisie* was now firmly on the side of order. On 29 November the burghers of the city presented an address to Windischgratz thanking him for restoring the city and delivering them from the 'chains of terror-rule' (**148**).

Once Windischgratz had proclaimed martial law in Vienna the way was open to a complete counter-revolution throughout the Empire. The reaction was implemented by Windischgratz's brother-in-law, Schwarzenberg, who was appointed prime minister on 21 November 1848. The Constituent Assembly had already retreated to Kromeriz during the October scare. It continued its deliberations until March 1849 but it had become 'quite isolated from the turn of events' (**146**) and it was largely ignored by Schwarzenberg's government. The rejuvenation of the dynasty was now imminent and in December 1848 the Court persuaded the feeble-minded Ferdinand to abdicate. He was succeeded by his nephew, Franz-Josef, who was imbued with the dynastic ideal which was in direct accord with the disposition of Schwarzenberg, who wished to revive monarchical and thence bureaucratic authority. His government included Count Stadion*, as well as Alexander Bach*, who had adopted a distinctly conservative stance in contrast to the heady liberalism of the days of March.

The ability to revive dynastic moral authority depended, in part, on the success of the Imperial armies. The Italians were finally defeated at Novarra on 23 March 1849, only two weeks after Schwarzenberg had dissolved the assembly at Kromeriz. The Hungarians, however, were proving more difficult to subdue, and any protraction of the war against Hungary was likely to endanger the dynasty's moral recovery. It was probably this factor that induced Franz-Josef to accept Russian assistance. The Hungarians had already announced their refusal to recognise the monarchy in December 1848, and in January 1849, when Windischgratz's army occupied Budapest, Kossuth's government retreated to Debreczen, where Hungary was proclaimed an independent republic. Russian intervention was finally to seal Hungary's fate and tip the balance in favour of the forces of order. The Tsar may have feared unrest in his own territories – in Galicia or in Russian Poland – but more likely he simply believed it to be his 'duty to defend the security of the boundaries of Russia entrusted to [him] by God' (**177**) and simply to aid a fellow monarch. He was certainly suggestible to the theory of conspiracy and believed that the Hungarians had the backing of the Poles.

Whatever his reasons, Russian troops entered Hungary in June, and on 13 August the Hungarian army, under Gorgey, surrendered at Vilagos. Schwarzenberg now carried out a bloody repression: thirteen Hungarian commanders were executed and even the former prime minister, Count Batthyany, was shot. The Austrian commander who succeeded Windischgratz was General Haynau, whose brutal reputation came before him. He was responsible for 114 executions and 2000 imprisonments. Only Venice now remained independent of the authority of the monarchy. The revolution had all but run its course.

The liberal phase in the history of the Habsburg Empire had finally spluttered to a halt with the defeat of the Hungarians. Liberal constitutionalism had experienced a short and unsuccessful life. It was easily consumed by more vigorous national rivalries – a desire for Germanic ascendancy over Magyars as well as a Germanic-Magyar desire for ascendancy over Slavs. The willingness of the governor of Croatia, Jellacic, to pit his forces against the Magyars was of the same order as the Galician peasants' willingness to suppress the uprising of Polish nobles in 1846. Seen in this light it would appear that the achievements of the revolution were minimal, but there is no doubt that the revolutions of 1848 provided a great impetus in the development of the political life of the subject peoples of the Empire (**146**). Thus the events of 1848 were formative for the Italians in 1859–66 and for the Hungarians in 1867 when both these peoples achieved the essentials of their national political programmes – the Italians became a united nation and the Hungarians obtained autonomy within the Empire. In the social sphere the great enduring achievement of the revolution was the emancipation of the peasantry from the *Robot**. In the economic sphere the Empire became a single customs union by the abolition of all internal tariff barriers, but the revolution had little effect on the problems of industry; in particular the grievances of craftsmen and workers were not redressed despite their public appearance in the revolutionary uprisings. In the political-constitutional sphere the achievements of the revolution were negligible, and there is a case for saying that 'absolutism after 1848 was even more stringent and for a time more effective than before the revolution' (**146**). The Kromeriz Constitution was virtually ignored and all but superseded by the proposals of Stadion*. Equality before the law was now guaranteed, in theory if not in practice, but overall the power of the monarchy was stronger than ever after 1848, even though the rights of the nationalities – in education and public administration – were nominally recognised. Liberalism's timidity and ultimate defeat is explained by the fact that the forces arrayed against it were too vigorous. At the same time the link between liberalism and nationalism was now severely weakened. Liberalism, in fact, was giving way to more virulent conservative nationalism, of which German hatred of Slavism was the most sinister expression.

9 The German Lands

In discussing the 1848 revolutions it is not possible to talk of Germany in any coherent sense as a nation, as events followed different patterns in individual states. In Bavaria the agitation against Lola Montez pre-dated the news of the Paris revolution of February. There was a common theme, however, and that was the emergence of the new liberalism. This was as true of the southern German states, like Baden and Bavaria, as it was of the more traditional and reactionary Prussia. In fact it could be said that the acquisition of the Rhineland by Prussia in 1815 was instrumental in dragging Prussia into modern history, because when Frederick William IV capitulated to the revolution in Berlin, he appointed Ludolf Camphausen and David Hansemann, two Rhineland businessmen, to head a liberal administration.

Although it was the German liberals who grabbed the headlines in 1848, there were other important groups who were active in the revolution and they should not be overlooked. The liberal movement was essentially, as it was elsewhere in Europe, the product of middle-class ambition, and the German revolutions have been quite rightly explained in terms of a bourgeois demand for 'proper participation . . . in the construction of political life' (**127**). In those states where the liberal opposition came to power – Baden, Wurttemburg, Darmstadt, Nassau, Kassell, Saxony, Hanover and Prussia – the middle classes were demanding 'greater freedom of action, legal safeguards, political participation . . . and . . . national unity' (**119**). This stemmed, primarily, from a lack of political opportunity for the middle classes. In particular, they felt that they were unable to gain public positions within their respective states that were commensurate with their abilities and education. At the same time, the middle classes were exasperated with arbitrary bureaucracy (**115**), and the formation of a national state seemed to be a way in which their hopes could be realised. In addition to the middle-class liberal thrust there were other social-political forces at work, although historians are far less certain about their exact significance.

It should be remembered that in the 1840s some two-thirds of the

German population were still engaged in agriculture. Grievances related to the land and the remnants of feudal oppression were exacerbated by the problems of overpopulation (see above, Chapter 4). These grievances were especially felt in the Black Forest areas of the Odenwald, Briegau and Mulheim (**121**). Peasant discontent was not directed towards the same ends as middle-class liberal activity, but the violence of the peasant uprisings undoubtedly had an effect in frightening governments. The governments themselves also suffered from severe internal weaknesses and there is a sense in which the revolutions were due 'not only to the scope and character of the pressures' coming from below but also to an 'actual decline in the flexibility, autonomy and morale of the political elites themselves' (**53**).

Unrest in the towns and cities among workers and artisans was also of some importance, but the precise character of that unrest is more difficult to establish. German workers – artisans and new factory proletarians – were active in 1848, but their motives and the social and political meanings of their actions were often contradictory. The lamentable catalogue of social misery that was amassed by the Marxist historian, Kuczynski, in the 1930s (**27**) has left its mark on other historians of that tradition, notably Eric Hobsbawm, who has given a prime role to the working class in the Berlin uprising of March 1848 (**23**) (see above, Chapter 5, p. 41). This interpretation is very much at odds with that of Stadelmann, who claims that the 'grievances about working conditions . . . did not remotely play the part that might have been expected from widespread cries of distress for social reform in the 1840s' (**127**). However, the danger of social upheaval was certainly recognised by contemporaries in the ruling elite [**doc. 3b**].

Thus, although the workers were reacting against change and much of the artisan programme was conservative in character, there is, nevertheless, a strong case for saying that 'social discontent had fired the revolution' (**118**). Peasant rioting and the fighting of workers and artisans on the barricades were strong contributory factors in forcing the existing rulers to concede to the demands of the liberals. The fact that the middle-class liberal reform movement and the workers' movement, with its many disparate and often conflicting strands, eventually diverged, does not lessen the role of the working classes in bringing about the initial concessions of March 1848. The German revolutions seem to have been generated by a mixture of motives that were distinct and separate for different social groups. Peasants were concerned with the removal of their feudal obligations. Artisans wished to retain the protection afforded to them by their traditional guilds which were in the process of being dismantled at the insistence of middle-class liberals. Finally, within the politically conscious layers of the middle class there was the desire to achieve constitutional reform (**121**).

The first clear manifestation of middle-class liberalism occurred at Mannheim on 27 February, and the usual liberal demands were articulated. This was quickly followed by a meeting of liberals at Heidelberg on 29 February, and on 5 March fifty-one liberals resolved to call a pre-parliament or *Vorparlament* which eventually sat at Frankfurt on 31 March. Its proceedings lasted until 4 April. The *Vorparlament* resolved that a Constituent Assembly should be elected by 'independent' citizens. No doubt the German liberals received reports from Paris, and like their liberal counterparts in Vienna were fearful of what they would have construed as mob rule: 'It is from Paris that the crowing of the Gallic cock will once more awaken Europe,' wrote Marx (**4**). Some states decided on a residence qualification for those intending to vote in the Assembly elections. In Baden, voting was based on a property qualification; artisans, journeymen, farm labourers and domestic servants were excluded from the franchise. Elsewhere, those in receipt of charity or poor relief were disqualified. This was the case in Cologne where 25,000 people (29 per cent of the population) were in receipt of relief (**132**). So exclusive were the voting qualifications in Cologne and Trier that the labour associations of those towns advocated boycotting the elections altogether, as a form of protest.

This perhaps helps to illustrate the disparate themes which run through the German revolutions, for it was in the Rhineland, and Cologne in particular, that the first cycles of capitalist-style unemployment were being experienced. The situation was essentially similar in Berlin where the *Rheberger*, a group of unemployed workers, was active in organising demonstrations (**121**). When the Frankfurt Assembly met in May 1848 it was petitioned by the Berlin workers, under the inspiration of Stephan Born*, for a programme of social reforms including a minimum wage, a maximum working day, rights of association, a progressive income tax, state education, free libraries and the regulation of the apprenticeship system.

However, the aspirations of the middle-class liberals who were now gathering at Frankfurt were far removed from the concerns of the Berlin and Cologne workers and artisans. The exclusive voting qualifications under which the elections had been conducted in many of the German states meant that the Assembly was largely middle-class in character. By far the greatest proportion of those elected were educated men, including some fifty professors and sixty secondary-school teachers, although they were outnumbered by officials and bureaucrats (**132**). Only one peasant and four artisans were elected. The Assembly was, in the end, nothing more than a reflection of both the rise of the middle class and more specifically of the discontent of a faction within that class, namely the official element: 68 per cent of the deputies were civil servants or officials and 2.5 per cent were businessmen (**132**). Clearly, the care with which the ground rules for the elections were designed indicates the wish of the German middle-class politicians to keep the pace of change within bounds, and certainly nothing more than the establishment of a constitutional monarchy was desired.

The election of the Frankfurt Assembly was primarily an extension of the movement for a more constitutional form of government within the individual states. Thus, although German liberalism was weakly organised before 1848, it had nonetheless already voiced its opinions. For example, Friedrich Hecker and Gustav Struve had instigated a liberal convention at Offenburg in September 1847, and a programme demanding abolition of censorship, trial by jury and the elimination of feudal restrictions was drawn up [**doc. 2a**]. A further convention of liberals met at Heppenheim a month later and put forward a similar programme of liberal demands. But there was no really co-ordinated liberal movement, and there is little evidence that there was any fundamental challenge to monarchy as a form of government from the German middle class in 1848. Only Ludwig of Bavaria lost his throne, and in Prussia it would be fair to say that Frederick William IV created his own difficulties. This is an important point to bear in mind when considering the reasons for the eventual failure of the revolutions. Although there were revolutionary uprisings, demonstrations, meetings and assemblies, as well as the formulation of political programmes, the existing regimes survived – 'the armies remained loyal and the administrations, despite changes in ministers, functioned without interruption' (**123**).

In Prussia, perhaps the most intriguing aspect of the situation was that the monarchy appeared, temporarily, to embrace the principles of the revolution. Why was this so? Why did one of the most traditional dynasties of Europe go along with the revolution and accede to its demands? There are at least two explanations. Firstly, the self-confidence of Prussian absolutism had already been seriously undermined in the previous year. Frederick William had become embroiled in the problems that had emanated from the financing of railway construction. During the 1840s he had been under pressure to find state funds for the building of the *Ostbahn*, a railway from Berlin into the *Junker* economic heartlands of east Prussia, which was vital to *Junker* economic survival. Such an undertaking would have required a substantial state loan, as well as a significant increase in taxation, and not even Prussian absolutism felt strong enough to raise taxation of this order without some representative backing. In 1820, the previous king, Frederick William III, had promised that any increase in the state debt would not be allowed without the approval of some representative body. Consequently, in 1847 Frederick William IV called a *United Diet*. Apart from representatives of the aristocracy, there were also bankers, merchants, professional men and provincial mayors. The *United Diet* put forward a set of classical liberal demands as a bargaining counter to the King's request to raise taxation. The situation was deadlocked and neither side was prepared to budge. Subsequently the *Diet* broke up, but the experience was not lost on the King. Prussian liberalism, by stubbornly opposing the King's demand for a loan for the *Ostbahn*, had shown that it was a force to be reckoned with. The second major factor which brought about Frederick William's ready capitulation in 1848 stemmed from conditions in Berlin. Early in March 1848, 400 workers were dismissed from Borsig's engineering works. This created a tense situation – tension heightened when news of Metternich's resignation reached the city on 18 March. Clashes between the populace and troops broke out. Frederick William announced his intention to grant reforms, and a crowd gathered in the palace courtyard, apparently in support of the King. However, troops in the royal household panicked and shots were fired. At this point craftsmen and workers took to the streets and erected barricades. Frederick William seems to have lost his nerve and decided to throw in his lot with the revolution. He paraded in the streets of Berlin, swathed in the German tricolor, announcing that 'Prussia merges into Germany.'

The March Days fighting was both victory and defeat for the advocates of reform. It was victory in the sense that the monarchy had been humiliated, and that Frederick William appointed liberal ministers on 29 March; but it was defeat in that it made the *Junkers* determined to crush the insurrection and it also persuaded the middle classes of the imminent danger of social revolution, pushing them over to the side of order. Moreover, it encouraged them to limit their political programme to minimal constitutional demands.

This preoccupation with legalities arising from the formation of the Frankfurt Assembly was the major concern of some historians writing in the 1940s (**37, 128**). Consequently, the activity of artisans and workers has been left to later generations of historians to demonstrate. The revolutions certainly signalled the release of the many pent-up grievances of the working classes. Urban discontent had centred around the grievances of the *Handwerker* throughout the 1840s. These craftsmen had long enjoyed independent status and were virtual aristocrats within their communities. However, the growth of free-market competition had prompted a number of German state governments to abolish many of the protectionist elements of the guild system, as was the case in Prussia in 1845 and in Hanover in 1847. *Handwerker* protests had already manifested themselves before 1848 – in the Palatinate in 1832 and in Silesia in 1844 – but it was the revolutionary year that unleashed the grievances of the artisan class.

German industry had suffered from problems of overproduction in 1847. The associated collapse of demand was followed by a tightening of credit controls by German banks and this in turn caused a rise in unemployment among factory workers, as well as a squeezing of many independent artisans who lost orders from the factories which they had been supplying. During the winter of 1847 there had already been many outbreaks of rioting and looting; and in Berlin angry workers stormed the palace of the Crown Prince. In Solingen, unemployed cutlers attacked iron foundries, while on the great rivers of the Rhine and the Danube dispossessed boatmen sabotaged steamships (**118**). This discontent carried on into 1848, and in August Stephan Born* formed the *Arbeiterverbruderung*, which was the first nationally based workers' organisation. The significance of these events should not be overestimated as 'only a minority of the skilled artisans had undertaken sustained political action. Their chief thought had been . . . to extract small improvements in their lives' (**124**). To this end workers and artisans formed their own assemblies, the two most important meeting in Hamburg and Frankfurt. From the programmes that appeared from these assemblies, it is clear that the overriding concern of the artisanate was the growth of factory production and the abolition of the guilds. They certainly wanted to retain their privileged status within the working class as a whole by defending the guild system, but this of course put them at odds with the middle-class liberals who met at Frankfurt (**133**). In general terms, it would seem that the worker movement was defensive in its impetus, seeking to maintain a world that was under threat as a consequence of the growth of modern methods of factory production. This defensive attitude manifested itself in numerous ways, not only in the programmes of the worker assemblies but also in the anti-Semitic sentiments that were expressed by many sections of the artisanate. A revealing example is provided by the *Handwerker* of Leipzig: 'There is no greater enemy of the petty *bourgeoisie* and of the labouring classes, no greater enemy of the solidarity of the small trades than these aliens [i.e. Jews]. . . . Their heart is the money bag' (quoted in **133**).

The Industrial Code* put forward by the Artisan Congress was generally opposed to free enterprise. The Frankfurt Assembly, on the other hand, saw political and economic freedom as inseparable principles. Consequently, it rejected the Industrial Code, and in the long run this may help to explain why the *Handwerker* welcomed the revival of monarchy in the German states (**133**).

The deliberations of the two liberal middle-class assemblies – the one at Frankfurt and the other at Berlin – still have to be considered. The Frankfurt Assembly was concerned with the formation of a nation state. Three principal solutions were suggested. A minority of deputies demanded the formation of a democratic republic. Others, like Heinrich von Gagern, wanted to retain the essentially federal element of the existing *Bund*. This view was supported by many of the Catholic representatives, who were suspicious of anything that smacked of Prussian secularism. Finally, there were Prussian conservatives, like von Radowitz*, who were more concerned with the integrity of Prussia than with a united Germany. The Frankfurt Assembly was fraught with division and uncertainty, not only over the form of government – democratic-republican, federal, secular – but also over the territorial extent of the new Germany. Should it encompass all the German lands, including those currently in the Habsburg Empire? Or should it only include those states that formed the core of the existing German *Bund* and exclude German Austria?

These political divisions were underpinned by a general fear of social revolution. German Marxist historians have argued that the Frankfurt Assembly aimed to stifle the working-class revolution. The liberals, in their view, eschewed democracy in favour of an alliance with the old dynasties in which the the middle class became a 'subordinate partner in an illiberal system of governance' (**136**). The Assembly was undoubtedly divided on many fundamental issues, not least the question of the power of the German Emperor or King, and almost half the deputies were in favour of the King possessing an absolute veto (**136**). This was hardly typical liberalism in any recognisable western European sense. So, although the Frankfurt liberals espoused general aspects of European liberalism – equality before the law, careers open to talent, inviolability of personal liberty, freedom of the press – they were still wedded to notions of social and political deference. Thus they balked when demands to abolish aristocratic privilege were put forward. 'The truth is that they were at least as strongly opposed to democracy as they were to the old regime, and their challenge to the latter should not be overstated' (**136**).

Not only was there little basis for agreement among the Frankfurt deputies; they did not really possess the authority to make their decisions effective. The powers of both assemblies – Frankfurt and Berlin – were never really defined; and the counter-revolution is perhaps best understood in terms of the fact that the old dynasties 'reasserted powers which may have been dormant but never surrendered' (**123**). This lack of real authority was illustrated in the Polish and Schleswig-Holstein questions. Taking the Polish question first, it should be remembered that at the Congress of Vienna in 1815 Prussia had obtained the Duchy of Posen. Some Prussian liberals believed that Posen should be surrendered in order to facilitate the formation of a Polish state. This was certainly not the view taken by the majority of the Frankfurt liberals, who were more concerned with the 700,000 Germans who lived in the Duchy. The 'temptation' (**4**) of the German liberals to absorb Posen was too great; and on 2 May 1848 the Assembly voted 342 to forty-one in favour of this. It was perhaps one of the few issues on which there was virtual unanimity. Such an ambition stemmed from long-established assumptions about German cultural superiority in central Europe (**175**), and, no doubt, from a desire to maintain a buffer between Germany and the real enemy of liberalism – Russia. Effectively, therefore, the Frankfurt Assembly merely supported the traditional aims of Prussian foreign policy.

In the case of Schleswig-Holstein, not only was the ineffectiveness of the Frankfurt Assembly demonstrated but so too was the weakness of Prussia in international affairs. The diplomatic detail of the Schleswig-Holstein question is long and complex, but the episode in 1848 displayed the dilemma of the Frankfurt nationalists in respect of national boundaries. The two duchies had long been claimed by the Danish King, while Prussia had always supported the claims of the Duke of Augustenburg. The intention of the King of Denmark, Frederick VII, to absorb the two duchies within the Danish kingdom brought a noisy protest from the Frankfurt liberals. They looked to Prussia to defend the German speakers in the two duchies. Prussia in fact occupied the two provinces between April and May 1848, but this action brought opposition from both Russia and Britain, who feared an extension of Prussian power into the Baltic and North Seas respectively. Prussian acceptance of the armistice at Malmo on 26 August and the withdrawal of General Wrangel's troops demonstrated the extent to which Prussia was still the junior partner in the alliance which had combined against Napoleon in 1814 and had dictated the terms of the Settlement of 1815.

It also showed that the German question was a European question, in the sense that a strong Germany in central Europe could affect the balance of power as a whole. At one level Lord Palmerston, the British Foreign Secretary, welcomed the strengthening of Prussia's role in Germany and central Europe, since she could act as a bulwark against both French and Russian rivalries. But Britain did not wish to see the continent dominated by a Germany that was too strong, lest that restrict Britain in her extra-European role as a world sea-power. Perhaps Russian opposition was more significant, since the Tsar was bitterly opposed to the revolutions and was eventually to lend his support to Austria in suppressing the Hungarian uprising. Russian support for Austria was an implicit repudiation of Prussian claims to exert hegemony in Germany. The capitulation of Prussia at Malmo demonstrated the complexity of the German question and at the same time estranged the Frankfurt liberals from the Prussian state. The Frankfurt deputies regarded the withdrawal from Schleswig-Holstein as a treacherous betrayal of the German national cause (**128**). But there was also a sense in which the issue damaged the Frankfurt liberals more than it damaged Prussia, and this is the second major aspect of the crisis: 'The ill-fated Malmo armistice dealt a very serious blow to the authority of the Frankfurt Parliament' (**111**). The episode revealed quite starkly that Frankfurt had no means of conducting an independent foreign policy. Power still lay in Vienna and Berlin, and the Assembly looked to Prussia to conduct foreign policy by proxy on behalf of the nebulous German national movement. The isolation of the Frankfurt Assembly is further demonstrated by recalling that only the USA gave it diplomatic recognition. Not even the French Republic could lend its support to Frankfurt over the question of the two duchies. The Schleswig-Holstein question represents a turning-point in the history of the German revolutions. Prussia's commitment to German nationalism had never been convincing, any more than Frederick William's overtures to liberalism. Now Prussia was to move decisively against the revolution.

In the same month that Prussia had been forced to accept the armistice at Malmo, the *Junkerparlament* meeting in Berlin resolved to form a League for King and Country, and declared its open opposition to the Prussian Assembly which was also meeting in Berlin. By October the King had swung back to a more traditional position and dismissed his liberal ministers. The Berlin Assembly was moved out of the capital to Brandenburg in November, only to be dissolved the following month. The reaction brought about by the new Minister of the Interior, Otto von Manteuffel, marked a revival of monarchical confidence. It also marked the beginning of the end of Prussian liberalism.

Prussia's failure over Schleswig-Holstein had repercussions in Frankfurt. The Assembly had never come to terms with the social problems which had initially activated the workers in March 1848. The workers' demands for restoration of the guild system, and for compulsory elementary education as well as a progressive income tax, went much too far for the professors and officials of the National Assembly. They had not appreciated the realities of power, believing that solutions lay 'through discussion and by agreement' (**37**). Faced with the politics of confrontation and ultimatum, they froze. Thus a popular demand for refusal to pay income tax in November 1848 was rejected by the Assembly, thereby displaying once again the liberals' inability to deal with the social question. This failure had been constant, but now, with the débâcle over Schleswig-Holstein, it had spread to the national question as well, with the consequence that the Frankfurt liberals became increasingly politically isolated.

The Frankfurt Assembly continued to debate the German Constitution until well into 1849 and eventually, in March, offered the crown of a united Germany to Frederick William IV of Prussia. Although not rejecting the crown outright, the Prussian King claimed that he could not accept it unless with the 'voluntary assent of the Crowned Princes and the free states'. Frederick William was wedded to tradition, and regarded Prussia as Austria's junior; it was out of 'respect for Austria' (**37**) that he rejected the crown. This rejection signalled the break-up of the Assembly: the Prussian deputies withdrew and the Kings of Bavaria, Wurttemburg and Saxony refused to recognise the Constitution. The plight of the Frankfurt Assembly was now clear. It had no means of enforcing any of its decisions. Its existence had always been at the mercy of the King of Prussia and the German princes. The forces of reaction were now irrevocably in the ascendant.

Frederick William's involvement was not at end, however. He still believed, with some prompting from von Radowitz*, that it was possible to achieve a form of unitary German state under Prussian hegemony. To this end a meeting was held at Erfurt, attended by representatives from Prussia, Bavaria, Hanover and Saxony. The so-called Erfurt Union met with the approval of the right-wing and centre members of the old Frankfurt Assembly, who declared their support for it at Gotha in June 1850. However, Bavaria declared herself unwilling to sign the 'Erfurt Treaty', and Frederick William failed to capitalise on the support of Hanover and Saxony. The failure of Frederick William to assert Prussian leadership over the smaller German states was also apparent in the matter of Hesse-Kassel. The Elector of Hesse-Kassel was faced with a recalcitrant local *Diet* that had refused to vote him taxation. The Elector withdrew to Frankfurt and appealed to the reconstituted German *Diet* which Schwarzenberg, the new Austrian Chancellor, had feverishly been attempting to regenerate. The appeal of the Elector was a golden opportunity for Schwarzenberg to reassert Austrian influence in Germany. Troops were mobilised and the rebellion swiftly quelled. The isolation of Prussia was complete, since the Tsar assured Schwarzenberg that if Prussia opposed the action carried out in Hesse-Kassel by Austria and her new-found allies, Bavaria and Wurttemburg, then Russia would be prepared to provide military support for the counter-revolution (**111**).

The case of Hesse-Kassel, like that of Schleswig-Holstein, demonstrates the impotence of Prussia in international affairs at this time and the innate conservatism of Frederick William IV. If the pendulum had been swinging in favour of Prussia during the 1840s, it began rapidly swinging back in favour of Austria during 1849 and 1850. By the latter year, with the agreements at Olmutz, Austrian recovery was assured. Prussia accepted the dissolution of the Erfurt Union and agreed to the restoration of the *Bund* under the terms of the Federal Act of 1815 which reasserted the basis of Austrian primacy in German affairs. Schwarzenberg had won a famous victory and succeeded in virtually putting the clock back. Although later history showed this victory to be temporary, it was nonetheless a humiliating defeat for Prussia and marked the extinction of the flame of liberal nationalism.

The revolution failed because there was no common ground among the revolutionaries. On the one hand the artisans, workers and peasants were untouched by the abstractions of middle-class liberalism. On the other, the German *bourgeoisie*, petrified by the uprisings of workers in March 1848 and the even more radical outbreaks in Elberfeld and the Rhineland generally in May 1849, gravitated instinctively to the side of property and order (**118**). The revolution was also unable to produce any leaders of enduring substance. Almost all those who participated in the assemblies lacked political experience; and before a year was out the '"trees of liberty" planted by them had withered away' (**37**). At the same time it should be remembered that there were so many different locations of revolutionary activity – Berlin, Frankfurt, Vienna – that it was extremely difficult for the revolutionaries to co-operate in any concerted way. Yet the ultimate reason for the failure of the revolution was that German society was both intensely hierarchical (**118**) and 'deeply conservative in structure and outlook' (**111**). The middle class was still numerically small and this explains, in part, the timidity of German liberalism. It certainly explains the ease with which the counter-revolution was able to reassert the rule of the princes.

10 The Italian Peninsula

The revolutions in Italy began in January 1848. On 3 January the first clashes between the Milanese and the Austrian garrison took place. At Leghorn in Tuscany there was an uprising on 6 January led by the democrats La Cecilia, Fabrizi and Guerazzi*. This was, in fact, the climax of a long period of social and political unrest which had been rumbling from September 1847 onwards (**170**). Between 12 and 27 January there was an uprising in Palermo, to which Ferdinand II responded on the 29th by granting constitutional concessions. In Tuscany the Grand Duke Leopold issued a constitution and appointed Ridolfi and Serristori, leading liberals, to government posts. Thus, revolution had already made considerable headway on the peninsula even before Louis Philippe abdicated in France. This helps to strengthen the argument that the revolutions were caused by broad-scale factors that were working at a European level and were not dependent, therefore, in every case, on the formative example of the French.

There are three main themes to be considered in the Italian revolutions. Firstly, there was the revolution against Austrian rule in Lombardy and Venetia which escalated into a war involving the other Italian states; secondly, a general demand for a more liberal and in some cases more democratic form of government in individual states; and thirdly, urban craftsmen and workers (and to a lesser extent the profoundly oppressed peasantry) hoped to bring about a social revolution.

Taking the social revolution first, it is important to recognise that the Italian economy was experiencing both growth and decay simultaneously. The peninsula possessed a relatively large number of urban centres, but apart from Milan and Turin, which had grown quite quickly in the first half of the nineteenth century, the other cities often exhibited the features of economic stagnation and decay. The populations of Venice and Palermo had actually fallen since the Restoration. In almost all Italian cities, whether growing or stagnating, economic life was structured around the activities of the *petite bourgeoisie*. In Genoa in 1838 there were 21,000 masters and apprentices, together with 64,000 shopkeepers and traders, out of a total of population of 114,000. The upper middle class of merchants and bankers, together with the urban intelligentsia, formed a small but visible elite.

For the mass of the city populations, living standards generally declined in the decades after 1810 and the sanitary conditions of Italian cities were recognised as some of the worst in Europe: in Naples in the 1840s the life expectancy of those living in the central districts was only twenty-four years. In 1848 risings seem to have occurred in those cities where there was an acute physical separation between the social elite and the poor. Thus, wherever there was marked social zoning in residence patterns – in Palermo, Venice, Naples and Rome – there were revolutionary outbreaks. In Turin there was no popular uprising in 1848, and this has been attributed to the remarkable social cohesion that existed in the city where rich and poor could be found living in different apartments of the same building (**172**). Although the urban culture of Italy was extremely well developed, it should also be recognised that, of all the regions of Europe, with the exception of Russia and the Iberian peninsula, it had the largest proportion of its population still employed in agriculture. Conditions in agriculture are extremely important for understanding the initial discontents of 1848. Between 1820 and 1870 Italian agriculture endured a long crisis in which the 1840s was one of the most depressed decades. The Italian peasantry were largely untouched by the political programmes of the *Risorgimento*, but their economic condition encouraged them to acts of disorder, violence, riot and arson.

Italian agriculture was strikingly inefficient (**14, 173**) and it was particularly vulnerable to foreign competition in the years immediately before 1848. At the same time there was considerable pressure to transform Italy's basically feudal agricultural system into something that was much more recognisably capitalist. The most extensive changes had been wrought in the northern states of Piedmont, Lombardy and Venetia. But even here the two agricultural systems of feudalism and capitalism co-existed. For example, in the district of Bologna there were about 45,000 day labourers, known as *braccianti*, who worked for wages. There were also an equal number of peasant landholders or *mezzadri*, who were obliged to work a number of contractual days for local landowners. In the north-western districts of the Dolomites, there was a class of peasant producers, known as *livello*, who worked small plots on long-term leases. The peasants here produced potatoes, cereals and chestnuts as well as wine, on a largely subsistence basis. In the more fertile areas of the Veneto more capitalist-style operations were carried out, such as the growing of mulberry trees for silk production. Thus even in the developed north, there were a multitude of production modes existing side by side and in some areas there were pockets of proto-industry such as domestic silk manufacture, often carried out by peasant women. But in almost all regions, agriculture alone was not strong enough to sustain peasant life, and temporary seasonal migrations to the towns were becoming a normal part of the peasant experience. Employment in the building trades or on the construction of the Milan to Venice railway became an increasingly attractive alternative to the marginal nature of life in the countryside. Peasant grievances in Lombardy and Venetia were manifold – resentment of Habsburg conscription and taxation was compounded by the disastrous harvests of 1845 and 1846. Peasant discontent had in fact been mounting throughout 1846 and 1847, but Habsburg administration was slow to respond, despite petitions from the Venice business community to place an embargo on grain exports in March 1847 (**163**).

The extent of privation in the countryside was so great that when the initial outbreaks of unrest exploded at the beginning of 1848 the peasants descended upon the provincial cities of upper Lombardy, including Como, Monza, Lecco and Sondrio. At Milan, an Austrian officer in the garrison wrote that 'the city was surrounded by uproarious peasants who came running in their thousands, shooting at the soldiers' (quoted in **153**). Their action was spontaneous and was motivated by a desire to drive the Habsburg troops out and to bring an end to Habsburg taxation and conscription (**174**). Thus although the urban classes were often the vanguard of the original revolutionary surge, the peasants were quick to come to the aid of the townspeople. This was equally true in the south, where agriculture was extremely backward. In the Palermo uprising, craftsmen were in the front line but peasants were quickly on the scene (**172**).

Conditions in the countryside also rebounded upon the towns. Vulnerability to foreign competition and organisational backwardness meant that agricultural products were subject to violent price fluctuations in urban markets. In fact these price fluctuations were some of the most extreme in Europe. The price fluctuations at Udine market were over 59 per cent between 1841 and 1850 and the total price fluctuation of maize was over 58 per cent (**5**), [**doc. 4**]. In the Venice market the price of wheat almost doubled between 1845 and 1847 and the price of maize increased by 77 per cent (**174**) [**doc. 4b**]. Naturally enough there had been a number of city riots during the 1840s and these had increased in frequency between February and March 1847. There had also been outbreaks of Luddism* in Rome as well as demands from the Tuscan peasants for a reduction in the number of their contractual labour days (**9**).

But perhaps the most striking feature of the towns was the growing division between the *bourgeoisie* of merchants and traders on the one hand and the craftsmen on the other. In Leghorn an uprising of workers was confronted by an essentially *petit bourgeois* civic guard (**23**); and in Naples, although the *bourgeoisie* initially welcomed the uprising since it added impetus to their demands for a constitution, they were quick to plead for the formation of a civic guard, a desire that was, according to one contemporary, 'born of the eternal diffidence of the owner towards the non-owner' (quoted in **172**). The Papal States, too, experienced outbreaks of worker discontent where there was considerable poverty and unemployment. Count Terenzio Mamiani's government, although apparently committed to the establishment of public workshops, was unable to fund such projects. Consequently, the workers of Rome established a number of radical clubs demanding higher taxation as a means of tackling poverty. Just like many of the French and German workers, then, the Italian workers and peasants were motivated by a complex of economic grievances. In the short run, the fact that their grievances did not coincide with those of the middle classes did not matter, as all the 'traditional divisions and parochial jealousies appeared to be submerged by a general desire to evict the foreigner' (**172**). In the long run, however, the gap between bourgeois ambition and worker-peasant hope was to lead to the disintegration of revolutionary unity.

Turning now to the question of political demands, there were two separate but overlapping campaigns. There was demand for reform within the individual states, combined with a demand to expel Austria and unite the Italian states. Both movements emanated from the urban intelligentsia, and within the individual states there were both liberal and democratic movements. Liberal reform movements existed in almost all the Italian states, but especially in the northern ones, where there was a well-developed middle class with entrepreneurial and commercial interests. In Lombardy, the writings of Cattaneo, a republican, were specifically addressed to the urban *bourgeoisie*, and in Piedmont the works of Balbo, D'Azeglio* and Petitti, all moderate reformers, served to raise the hope of constitutional reform.

The aspirations of the moderates had already received some

encouragement with the election of Pope Pius IX in 1846. For whatever reasons Pius IX trod the path of liberal reform when he succeeded Gregory XVI, and the effect of his actions reverberated throughout the length and breadth of the peninsula. On becoming Pope, Pius appointed the liberal-minded Cardinal Gizzi as Secretary of State. The press laws were relaxed and subsequently a Council of State with secular representatives was allowed to share power with the College of Cardinals (**30**). When the Council eventually met in November 1847, Pius's caution about the forces he had inadvertently unleashed was already becoming apparent and he informed the new body that the council would 'not detract minimally from the sovereignty of the pontificate' (quoted in **172**).

But it was too late. Liberal hopes had been raised and democratic pressures were forcing governments elsewhere on the peninsula into making concessions. The democrats had been active throughout the 1830s and 1840s and they had support from every social class, even though that support was, in numerical terms, rather small. Now, in the years after 1846, democratic radicals could seek support among urban craftsmen and bourgeois intellectuals as well as from rural peasants in such areas as Basilicata, Calabria and Romagna (**165**). Thus, when the Pope made his vital concessions, he brought about demands for reforms elsewhere. In ultra-conservative Tuscany, the moderate reformers were in danger of losing 'control of a situation they themselves had created' (**172**). Such was the excitement engendered by this bout of Papal liberalism that Radetzky*, commander of the Austrian forces in Venetia, frightened by its implications, ordered the occupation of the city of Ferrara even though it lay inside the Papal States. The Pope appealed to Charles Albert, the King of Piedmont, for protection. The actions of this enigmatic ruler are interesting. He was the last monarch on the peninsula to grant a constitution and he was not disposed to accept liberal reform or any dilution of his personal power. On the other hand, he was ambitious for Piedmontese aggrandisement and, unlike Frederick William IV of Prussia, he was prepared, ultimately, to make war on Austria.

Charles Albert's willingness to confront the Austrians made him, temporarily, the champion of the patriots, just as the Pope had become the champion of the liberals. At this stage events in Lombardy and Venetia were decisive. In Milan and Venice it had been workers and craftsmen who had started the revolution (**163, 172**), with the arsenal workers in Venice playing a decisive role (**163, 174**). The leaderships of these two revolutions were, however, rather indecisive. In Milan, Cattaneo, a republican, became the leading member of the revolutionary committee and he had, at first, doubted the wisdom of fighting the Austrian garrison (**30**). He was to be surprised by events, since on 22 March Radetzky* decided to evacuate the city and withdraw his troops to the fortresses of the Quadrilateral*. The moderates in Milan now pressed for Piedmontese intervention, 'not only against the Austrians, but against the violent revolutionary elements in their own city' (**30**). Charles Albert prevaricated and this was due, for the most part, to his conservative nature, as he did not wish to be identified with the revolution. Nevertheless, the pressure of liberal nationalism, not only in Lombardy but also from his own ministers, principally Cavour, was so great that Charles Albert resolved in favour of military intervention. Even now, however, he insisted on the holding of a plebiscite to secure Lombard acceptance of his leadership (**169**). The Lombard moderates were agreeable and the plebiscite was duly held on 12 May 1848. Cattaneo and the republican democrats were now completely isolated. Cattaneo had hankered for the formation of an independent Lombard republic that would eventually become a member of a federated Italian state: 'Italy is physically and historically federalist,' he claimed. He also believed that French support would be forthcoming, but he had not reckoned with the caution of Lamartine and the Provisional Government in Paris. Lamartine had already made the non-interventionist position of the Second Republic clear in his *Manifesto to Europe* (see above, pp. 56–7). The plebiscite in Lombardy recorded a majority in favour of fusion with Piedmont and acceptance of Charles Albert's leadership.

In Venice events had already taken a decisive turn. Workers in the arsenal had rioted and killed the proprietor, Marinovich, and on 22 March Daniele Manin* had declared Venice a republic. The revolution, initially, seemed to sweep everything before it, gaining the support of all classes including the clergy; even the Bishop of Padua advocated taking up arms against the Austrians (**163**). However, as at Milan, the government of the Venetian Republic was made up of bourgeois moderates (**172**). It was not surprising, therefore, that the new Venetian government looked for support from Piedmont, especially once the Austrians had mounted a naval blockade against Venice itself.

In Piedmont Charles Albert was unenthusiastically associating himself with the national cause for fear that the radical forces might subsume the revolution or that the French might intervene on behalf of the Lombards. It was against this background that he embarked on the military campaign against Austria. The war turned out to be a disaster, for Charles Albert's army was poorly led and badly supplied (**169**). Moreover, the political divisions of Italy became apparent as early as April when the Pope refused to support the war, and this completed the 'disillusion of the patriots' (**30**). In particular it discredited Gioberti* and those who had advocated a federalist Italy under the presidency of the Pope. The Pope's declaration was effectively the first blow for the counter-revolution as it inspired the King of the Two Sicilies, Ferdinand, to repossess his capital city, Naples, by military force. He still accepted the constitution but he abolished the Civic Guard and called his troops back from the north of Italy in order to begin the reconquest of the island of Sicily. Thus even before the first major military encounter of the war at Custozza in July 1848, support for the war of liberation was breaking up.

Meanwhile the Austrians had begun a recovery. Windischgratz, the Habsburg commander in Bohemia, had regained control of Prague in June and this made it possible to send reinforcements to Radetzky*. The consequence of Charles Albert's procrastination was now to become clear. He had missed the opportunity to take advantage of Radetzky's weakened army whilst it was in retreat; now it had been reinforced with a further 30,000 men. It should not be thought, however, that Radetzky's suppression of the Lombardo-Venetian revolution and the defeat of Piedmont was a one-sided affair. The Habsburgs remained in a state of uncertainty, and Hummelauer, the Habsburg negotiator with Britain, was still seeking, right up until June, to gain Britain's co-operation as a mediator. Hummelauer, with the backing of the Habsburg Court, suggested the possibility of some measure of autonomy for Lombardy and Venetia (**44**). But the suppression of the revolt in Prague stiffened the resolve of the Habsburg Court, and the conciliatory Hummelauer was replaced by the much tougher Wessenberg. By 1 July the Court had come to accept the need to 'prosecute the war in Italy and leave its outcome to be settled in the field' (**148**).

Radetzky* now engaged the Italian forces along a line from Rivoli to Mantua and after several days of fighting defeated Charles Albert's army at Custozza (23–27 July). This victory demonstrated 'even more clearly than Prague that so long as the governments could rely on their armies they could sooner or later master the forces of upheaval' (**30**). Radetzky was now able to mount a complete counter-revolution in Lombardy. When the revolution in Milan had originally erupted in January, Lombard peasants had rushed to the city in support and were eager to join the Civic Guard. The city authorities, largely bourgeois moderates fearful of disorder, locked them out of the city. Radetzky* was now able to capitalise on these latent social divisions, and on 11 November he announced that the Austrian authorities would raise an extraordinary levy from those who had actively supported the revolution, as a kind of indemnity. This so-called 'war-tax' would have had the effect of exposing the urban revolutionary activists, especially when the military governor of Milan, Count Wimpffen, granted an amnesty to all those who were behaving with 'political propriety'. The revolutionary government of Milan was now beginning to lose confidence in face of the Habsburg counter-revolution.

The victory of the Habsburgs at Custozza did not by any means bring the revolution to an end. Indeed, in some quarters the defeat had the effect of intensifying democratic and radical pressure. In Genoa and Bologna, especially, support for republicanism was still strong, and in Tuscany and the Papal States democratic agitation led to the collapse of the moderate government of Capponi on 12 October. This marked the 'first success of the democrats in breaking the moderate monopoly of political power in the monarchical states' (**172**). The new republican government included Guerazzi*, leader of the revolutionary movement in Leghorn where there had been a major democratic uprising between 25 August and 4 September. In Rome, the assassination of the moderate politician Pellegrino Rossi persuaded the Pope to flee the city, which now fell under the control of the democrats. A new provisional government accepted a plan to elect a constituent assembly, and when the elections were held in January 1849 the republicans gained an overall majority. The Roman Republic was proclaimed in February 1849.

Rome now became the centre-stage of Italian politics. Mazzini* had returned to the city and the republicans sought to unite with Tuscany, but Guerazzi* was facing great difficulty in maintaining control of Florence. Republicanism was now becoming increasingly isolated, and with the defeat of the Piedmontese forces at Novarra in March 1849 the Florentine nobility called for the restoration of the Grand Duke Leopold. In the south, Ferdinand's troops had re-occupied Palermo on 15 May 1849. The Austrian re-conquest was now only a matter of time. The possibility of an Austrian foray into the Papal States prompted Louis Napoléon, President of the French Republic, to act pre-emptively. If the Napoleonic legend was to be revived, then France would have to overthrow the Vienna Settlement and this could partly be achieved by blocking Austria on the peninsula. General Cavaignac had already stationed 3500 French troops at Marseille in December 1848, but it was eventually troops under the command of General Oudinot that were despatched to Rome at the end of April, and the Roman Republic was brought to an end in June 1849. It has usually been argued that Louis Napoléon was guided by a desire to acquire clericalist support at home by being seen to be the defender of the papacy (**63, 65**). Whether this was the case, or whether he feared Austrian ascendancy, is not clear, but the effect was decisive: it all but drew the curtain on the revolutionary episode.

Only Venice remained in republican hands, but it had been under tight blockade since July 1848. When the city capitulated on 22 August 1849, the radical phase of the revolution was at an end. The Venetians had failed because of the resilience and tenacity of Radetzky*, and once General Nugent had regained control of Verona in May then the days of the Venetian Republic were numbered. But its collapse was not due simply to the fact that the forces of the counter-revolution were so durable. The bourgeois members of Manin's* republican government were so keen to avoid radical extremism that they resisted attempts to form a committee of public safety. Manin himself was too timid to be an effective leader, and his government did nothing to alleviate the privations that existed in the countryside. The abolition of the salt tax was the only social measure taken. All the republican leaders – Guerazzi* in Tuscany, Mazzini* in Rome and Manin in Venice – were democratic theorists. All of them were fearful of mob rule and they were as determined as their predecessors, the liberal constitutionalists, to maintain public order and the defence of property. A combination of timidity and political inexperience prepared the ground for their failure, and in the last resort military power provided the *coup de grâce* (**30**).

After his defeat at Novarra, Charles Albert abdicated from the throne of Piedmont. His successor quickly re-established royal authority. The national cause had inspired the nobility and the middle classes but it had failed to capture the imaginations of the peasants and the urban artisans whose identification with the revolution had only been a short-lived affair. These inherent social divisions, combined with the defence of the *status quo* by Britain and France, enabled the Habsburgs to recover their confidence and crush the revolution.

Part Four: Assessments and Consequences

If a survey for a political map of Europe had been carried out in 1845 and then repeated ten years later it would have revealed few differences. Not surprisingly, therefore, some historians have regarded the 1848 revolutions as failures, and have consequently focused their attention on finding explanations for their lack of success. The general conclusion has been that the revolutionaries failed to capitalise on their opportunities, because they were too idealistic and inexperienced (**37**, **128**). Related to this general conclusion is the view that the 1848 revolutions in some way arrested or retarded the natural course of history. This view derives support from the fact that within twenty years or so many of the aims of the revolutionaries had been realised – Italy and Germany were united and France became a republic.

To regard the 1848 revolutions as an unfortunate episode in an otherwise uniform march towards liberal government does not help the student who wishes to understand why the revolutions failed. Some historians have attributed failure to diffidence and weakness among the revolutionaries, and this has led them to stress the 'accidental' quality of the revolutions (**65**). Had the forces of order shown more determination, had Frederick William IV been sane (**128**), had Pius IX been typical of popes, then events would not have conspired to produce revolutions. The weakness of the forces of order, they argue, served to create a power vacuum in which the revolutionaries paraded with their flags and the liberal lawyers debated until such time as conservative forces reasserted themselves. There is much in this view since, with the exception of France, Bavaria, the Papal States and Tuscany, the existing governments were not actually deposed. Yet the weakness of the forces of order cannot be explained purely in terms of the frailty of certain individuals. If such an explanation is to be pursued, then the limp acceptance of events by Louis Philippe should be stressed, along with the ageing of Metternich and possibly the arrogance of Lola Montez in Bavaria. Such explanations hinge too much on individuals, and rely on the notion of 'accident'. Furthermore, it should be pointed out that the weakness of individual rulers was mirrored in the revolutionary camp. The revolutions did not produce a single politician of inspired genius, leadership, single-minded determination or ruthless cruelty. There were no Cromwells, no Robespierres, no Lenins.

All this debate is ultimately unhelpful. A more productive line of examination may be to consider the geographical extent of the revolutions and the common experiences of the affected area. A useful preliminary is to establish which countries were *not* affected by the revolutions. Generally speaking it was those countries on the extreme fringes of Europe that were least affected. Britain was a case in point: admittedly there was a large Chartist demonstration in London, but it was a tame affair compared with the determined violence that had marked the movement in the early 1840s. In the extreme east, Russia was unaffected and even found time to suppress revolutionary activity outside her immediate territory, in the Habsburg lands and Wallachia. The Scandinavian countries were unaffected, and in the south events in Sicily were of an extremely local character. Of the countries least affected, Britain, and to a lesser extent Belgium, were very advanced in industrial terms; at the other extreme, Russia was extremely backward, in fact largely feudal. Within the central area of Europe affected by the revolutions it is probably fair to say that France, Germany, northern Italy and to a lesser extent the Habsburg lands displayed the features of industrial progress and economic backwardness. All these regions were still prone to an agricultural crisis of the traditional type, namely a food shortage. Further, they were becoming prone to the financial cycles consistent with the development of capitalism which involved overproduction problems. The case of Britain is instructive here because Britain had experienced an industrial depression between 1838 and 1842. The continent did not experience such a crisis until 1846–49 and this coincided with a food crisis. It was the last time that Europe was to experience such a catastrophic food shortage, but it was made all the more serious by a new industrial crisis. Britain's economy, on the other hand, was already on the upturn by 1846. Obviously these economic difficulties alone do not explain the revolutions. Political discontent must also have been present. Significantly, both Britain and Belgium had been able to make timely concessions to the politically conscious layers of society – the middle classes – immediately before 1848 (see above, pp. 18–19).

Given the coincidence of two different types of economic crisis (**17**), it is necessary to consider the role of different social classes. In

France the dissatisfaction of the *bourgeoisie* with the railway policies of Guizot's* government is clear enough. Elsewhere, the determination of the middle class, especially in Germany, to stave off the threat of social revolution from the lower classes, was an indication not only of differing interests but also of the fact that the economic crisis of 1846–47 affected different classes in different ways. As economic privations abated, so any cohesion that the revolutionaries might have had began to disintegrate. This is abundantly clear in central Europe, where the peasantry lost interest in the revolution once the more oppressive features of the feudal system had been removed. In the Habsburg lands the peasants seem to have remained passive when Windischgratz subdued Prague and later besieged Vienna. In Lombardy the peasantry welcomed Radetzky's* return, probably feeling that the Milanese liberals had done nothing to deal with the economic problems of the countryside.

In France the role of the peasantry is less clear. Although there is much to be said for the argument that the Second Republic did nothing for the peasantry except impose the hated 45-centime tax (**18**), it cannot be said that the French peasantry stood exclusively on the side of conservatism and traditional order as represented by Louis Napoléon. The peasantry were divided and there was considerable peasant resistance to the *coup d'état* of December 1851 (**79, 101**).

Ultimately, the most serious social divisions that threatened the fabric of society manifested themselves in the towns and the cities. This was clearly demonstrated in Paris in June 1848 and in Vienna in October. In the German states too, middle-class fears of the danger of further social revolution drove them to policies of moderation so that at least they might appear to be the legitimate heirs of the governments of the princes. In France republicans were also inclined to pursue cautious policies and this was exhibited in Lamartine's obsession with foreign policy. He hoped to lay the ghost of war and Napoleonic expansion. This caution was also revealed in the pedantic legalism of the Frankfurt Assembly. The working-class movements and the organisations of the radical left were not, at this time, sufficiently well developed to force social and political changes in their favour. It is such divisions of interest, between the respectable middle class and the tradesmen on the one hand and the craftsmen and workers on the other, that provide the central explanation of the long-term failure of the revolutions. When these revolutions first broke out, the different expectations of the various social and political groupings did not matter. As they progressed, however, so the different expectations became divisive, and once the cohesion of the revolutionary groups had been impaired the way was open to counter-revolution.

The revolutions failed not just because of social conflicts. They also failed because of the policies pursued by Britain and Russia. British and Russian opposition to Prussia's attempted take-over of Schleswig-Holstein helped to discredit Prussia in the eyes of the liberal-nationalists at Frankfurt. Further, Britain's diffident policies in relation to Italy ultimately facilitated Austria's revival on the peninsula. British diplomacy was directed towards the maintenance of the *status quo* in Europe, and in this sense Austria was Britain's factotum in continental affairs. Perhaps, too, Britain could not openly support Italian claims for independence because such action might have encouraged Irish nationalism (**19, 44**). It was ironic, then, that although the success of the British middle-class reformers in 1846 had encouraged the Banqueteers and the Dynastic Opposition* in France, British diplomacy was still bent on the preservation of order and stability in Europe. This was the paradox of the British position – a socially and politically advanced state which tended to ally itself with the forces of order and reaction. Russia's position was more straightforward. Her assistance to Austria in suppressing the Magyar revolution stemmed from an unwavering adherence to the principles of dynasticism and a fear that revolution in territories so close to her own frontiers might encourage similar movements among her own disaffected subjects, principally the Poles (**175, 177**).

Following on from the reaction against the revolutions, there grew up in subsequent decades a more successful form of authoritarian government in France, Prussia and the Habsburg monarchy. In France Napoleon III was able to achieve a degree of political manipulation and control that was all the more surprising since he allowed universal male suffrage. The use of a democratic franchise for essentially conservative purposes was in its own way revolutionary because, before 1848, those who had advocated universal suffrage had done so in the belief that it would deliver their societies from the whims of monarchs and autocrats. On the other hand, it could be argued that the establishment of universal suffrage was one of the positive gains of the 1848 revolutions. Perhaps Louis Napoléon was aware of the need to recognise the demands of 1848. The regime made sure, though, through the control of the prefecture, that the first parliament of the Second Empire reflected the interests of the Bonapartist cause (**84**). It was not a puppet parliament, but it was not designed to cause too many difficulties for the Emperor.

In Prussia the resurgence of monarchical power achieved by Bismarck and William I was never seriously challenged. The way in which Bismarck, who was not a modern politician commanding the support of a pressure group or a party, flouted the parliamentary constitution of Prussia, created dangerous precedents for German history in the twentieth century. Bismarck was often impatient with parliamentary ways, although he was most solicitous towards monarchs; he was by inclination and training a courtier. Nevertheless, like Louis Napoléon, he recognised the value of the appearance of parliamentary government so long as conservative patronage and control were retained. Both regimes revealed something that must have been depressing for older generations of democrats. The achievement of parliamentary democracy did not radically change society as had been expected. Indeed, both German and French society retained a marked social hierarchy despite concessions to political democracy.

The continuation of such social hierarchies and the economic inequality on which they were based was a lesson that the mid-nineteenth-century generation of socialists did not forget. In fact, the 1848 revolutions destroyed the idealistic, almost mystical, belief that universal suffrage would bring with it social equality. Socialists were already critical of such a social-political equation and they could take some academic satisfaction from the events of June 1848. The 1848 revolutions may have helped to establish a link between the social conscience of intellectuals and the condition of the poorer classes. In the case of socialist intellectuals the 1848 revolutions strengthened their belief that revolution was the scientific and only logical outcome of historical change. For them, revolution was not, as it was to liberals, blind, illogical, destructive violence. Thus the 1848 revolutions provided political violence and conflict with a new intellectual credence and vitality.

If Prussia and France managed to establish a new successful authoritarianism, this was less than true in the Habsburg Empire. Admittedly the dynastic ideal had been invested with new life in the person of Franz-Josef, but the revival of the monarchy in the Habsburg Empire was not to prove so durable. Ultimately the Habsburgs were forced to accede to the demands for a measure of Hungarian autonomy in 1867. Nevertheless the temporary revival of the monarchy put an end to any liberal notions of a state that united all German-speaking peoples. This may not have been immediately apparent, for in the short run the Habsburg ascendancy over the

Hohenzollerns, as demonstrated at Olmutz, would have seemed to suggest the possibility of the continuation of Austrian influence in German affairs. In the long run, however, Prussia triumphed over Austria at Sadowa in 1866, with the result that Austria was banished from German affairs forever. The victory of Prussia at Sadowa was only one event in the political redefinition of central Europe between 1861 and 1866. It meant that Austria was excluded from those two areas – the Italian peninsula and the German states – that had made her so powerful since the Settlement of 1815. Consequently, in a search to recover lost prestige, the Habsburgs turned away from central Europe, seeking compensation instead in the Balkans. Eventually this was to mean a clash with Russia.

If, in those states which could be regarded as traditionally powerful – France, Prussia, Austria – a more successful authoritarian form of government was established, then the kingdom of Piedmont persevered with constitutional monarchy. Although Charles Albert had been reluctant to adopt constitutional ways, his successor, Victor Emmanuel II, was more ready to accept constitutionalism. This enabled the Piedmontese state to accommodate a growing commercial middle class, which in turn was able to harness Piedmont's economic ascendancy to unite the remainder of the peninsula. In this respect the role of Piedmont in the unification of Italy was similar to the role played by Prussia in Germany. The similarity does not end there, for in many ways Cavour, the Prime Minister of Piedmont after the fall of D'Azeglio*, approached the problem of the unification of Italy in the same manner that Bismarck tackled the question in Germany. Both recognised the importance of a manipulation of the balance of power in Europe in order to achieve specific national ends.

Cavour realised that Italian unification could only be achieved with outside help, which in the event was to come from France. Only then could Austria be expelled from the Italian peninsula. From Cavour's point of view this was a military and strategic consideration, but for the historian it demonstrates that the causes of the 1848 revolutions are to be found not only in deeply embedded social and economic problems, or even in political causes peculiar to individual states, but also in the broader political question of the nature of the Settlement of 1815. Given that the statesmen at Vienna had tried to provide a settlement for the whole of Europe, based on the principle of legitimism and denying the aspirations of the nationalities, then the 1848 revolutions have an international coherence. The liberal nationalists who were active immediately before 1848 had not especially appreciated this international dimension, with the possible exception of Palacky, whose attempts to restrain Czech nationalism, which was only a strand in a more general Slav nationalism, were derived from an appreciation of the significance of the balance of power, and specifically a fear of Russian expansion [**doc. 2c**]. The revolutionaries of 1848 were unable to change the balance of power and so their political aspirations were placed in a straitjacket that confined them to aiming for specific national autonomies without considering the ways in which these new nation states would relate to one another. In the hands of the post-1848 generation of nationalists, however, notably Bismarck and Cavour, nationalism was nothing if it did not manipulate the balance of power.

Nationalism did not fade away after the defeats of 1848, but it did change its style. Before 1848 nationalism, beyond the xenophobia and patriotism created in war, was, as a coherent body of ideas, largely the possession of an urban middle-class intelligentsia. They sought to provide a new and national basis for government that was established by consent between the people or the nation on the one hand, and the ruler or rulers on the other. Finding justification for their ideas in history, literature and elite culture, these middle-class propagandists had endeavoured to produce rational arguments for a reconstitution of the governments of Europe on national and liberal principles. After 1848, however, nationalism became an instrument used by conservative politicians to justify the continuation of monarchical power and to promote war. Above all, nationalism proved a powerful force for reconciling the internal class conflicts of the state. Its most skilful exponent was Bismarck who, by a series of patriotic wars, dispossessed the intellectuals of their academic and rational nationalism, making it popular, chauvinistic and aggressive. The nationalism of Bismarck was not the nationalism of Mazzini*.

The new nationalism of central Europe, represented primarily by German nationalism and to a lesser extent by Italian nationalism, was distinctly illiberal. It was a nationalism that became overtly racial in character. Admittedly, there had been cases of xenophobic nationalism before 1848 and there had also been pseudo-scientific claims for the superiority of certain racial groups over others. It was not until after 1848, however, that the scientific arguments became more powerful in their persuasiveness. In 1855 Alfred Gobineau had published his work on the natural inequality of races, and his submissions were given a deeper cutting edge by the apparent conclusions of Darwinian biology. Consequently, although the development was not a simple matter, there arose the view that the only viable form of state was one that was at least linguistically homogeneous if not racially 'pure'. Ultimately the survival of the multinational empires was at stake, since a reorganisation of the states of Europe on a national basis seemed, on scientific and moral grounds, inevitable. In terms of practical politics, the new racial nationalism engendered a Germanic hatred of Slavism. An instance of this hatred was seen much later in Bismarck's policy towards the Poles of eastern Prussia during the *Kulturkampf* in the 1880s. But in the long term the logic of the new nationalism spelt out the greatest danger to one group – European Jewry.

In international terms, nationalism was to redraw the map of Europe. This would not have been immediately apparent to a casual observer living in 1850. It would have seemed that the agreement at Olmutz between Austria and Prussia had effectively revived the Settlement of 1815 and at the same time revived the status of Austria. This was not so. Austria's revival was illusory. The survival of the Habsburg monarchy owed more to individuals – Radetzky*, Windischgratz, Schwarzenberg, Franz-Josef – than to any revitalisation of the system of government. More telling was the fact that the Habsburgs had only managed to defeat the Hungarians with the assistance of Russia. Coupled with this, it should be remembered that the European governments largely accepted the *coup d'état* of Louis Napoléon in France, which meant that the Settlement of 1815 had been implicitly rejected (**36**), [**doc. 1a**]. Ultimately this would open the way to the demise of the Habsburg Empire.

The economic consequences of the 1848 revolutions are not easy to tabulate. Economic progress is easy enough to discern, since the twenty-year period after the revolutions was a time of unprecedented economic growth. The early marks of expansion which had featured in the British and Belgian economies were now extended to France and the central European countries. Even Britain, which had enjoyed sustained growth before 1848, enjoyed yet greater economic progress in the years after 1820 (**23**). There is a danger, however, in attributing these developments directly to the 1848 revolutions. Obviously the breakdown of old institutional barriers and old customs facilitated economic growth: for instance, the expansion of Vienna from 444,000 inhabitants in 1850 to 726,000 in 1880 owed much to the immigration of people from other parts of the Empire. Such migration would not have been possible but for the abolition of feudal restrictions in the year of revolution. In Prussia, too, the last vestiges of feudalism were abolished by royal decree in 1850 and all remaining dues were translated into money rents. Large numbers of peasants (640,000) were able in time to buy their own plots. Institutional reform designed to facilitate economic development was one of the stronger trends to emerge in the years after 1848. In Piedmont the level of economic progress was high, and this was fostered by the new liberal governments of D'Azeglio* and Cavour. Even in the Kingdom of the Two Sicilies, which remained an autocratic monarchy, steps were taken to modernise agriculture and reclaim land (**173**). One thing is clear: the regimes that survived the 1848 revolutions were directly aware of the need to modernise their administration, even if they were not prepared to accept a dilution of their traditional forms of power.

The expansion of the European, and indeed, the world economy owed much to technological factors that were independent of the revolutions. The technical innovations of the railway and the telegraph enabled a broadening of the geographical area over which industrialism could prevail (**14, 23**). Migration also facilitated this process. Many Europeans were already on the move before 1848, as the result of land hunger and a failure of the European agricultural system, which were themselves contributory to the revolutionary upheaval. It has been estimated that emigration from Europe had averaged about 40,000 people *per annum* in the years before 1845, whereas the rate jumped to something over 200,000 *per annum* after 1848. Much of this movement, however, was made up of Irish, British and Scandinavian migration (**14**); in other words, it was migration from regions that did not play a major political role in the events of 1848. It would therefore be very difficult to establish any precise connections between the revolutionary upheaval and the subsequent pattern of European migrations.

It may well be that the establishment of strong and stable governments in France and Prussia encouraged the growth of industry and trade. Louis Napoléon's ascendancy was accompanied by a rise in stock market prices, though whether one was the cause of the other is impossible to tell. In the years after 1852 Louis Napoléon did follow policies that were conducive to economic expansion, and the Second Empire became noted for the emergence of new, dynamic and pushful entrepreneurs (**77**).

The expansion and consolidation of industrialism enhanced the significance of the middle classes. They became, in the more stable and efficient regimes of the post-1848 period, the residual legatees of the *ancien régime*. In Lombardy the breaking up of Church property and the suppression of old feudal privileges strengthened the growing commercial middle class (**173**). Eventually the interests of the

Lombards and the Piedmontese converged in favour of unity. In the German states the middle class, which was not as well developed as its counterparts in Britain and France, became increasingly politically conservative. This was probably a direct consequence of the 1848 revolutions. What had happened to an underdeveloped middle class in the German states in 1848 was that no sooner had it made its first incursion into politics than it faced opposition from the German artisan movement. Almost inevitably it became reactionary, never having the opportunity to be progressive. This had serious implications for Germany's later political development. In general, it was the European middle classes which made the most significant economic and political gains in the twenty years after 1848. Their ascendancy over other classes was marked, and in western and central Europe they were able, by the end of the century, to reconcile their own economic advantages with the dispossessed classes through various forms of the national-liberal state. Only in Russia did this not prove possible, and it was no coincidence that it was in Russia that the intellectual assertions of Marx's scientific socialism, which had derived so much impetus from the events of 1848, were to find their first practical application.

Part Five: Documents

documents 1a–c
The politics of conservatism and repression

(**a**) *After the defeat of Napoleon in 1815 the Great Powers were determined to preserve the territorial Settlement of Vienna. This meant that it was necessary to suppress all those 'progressive' ideas that had inspired the French Revolution. The Vienna Settlement was not, then, just a purely territorial arrangement.*

The High Contracting Parties, having engaged in the war which has just terminated, for the purpose of maintaining inviolably the arrangements settled at Paris last year, for the safety and interest of Europe, have judged it advisable to renew the said engagements by the present act, and to confirm them as mutually obligatory . . . particularly those by which Napoleon Bonaparte and his family . . . have been for ever excluded from Supreme Power in France, which exclusion the Contracting Powers bind themselves by the present act to maintain in full vigour, and, should it be necessary, with the whole of their forces. And as the same revolutionary principles which upheld the last criminal usurpation, might again, under other forms, convulse France, and thereby endanger the repose of other States; under these circumstances, the High Contracting Parties solemnly admitting it to be their duty to redouble their watchfulness for the tranquillity and interests of their people, engage, in case so unfortunate an event should again occur, to concert amongst themselves . . . the measures which they may judge necessary to be pursued for the safety of their respective States, and for the general tranquillity of Europe.

The Quadruple Alliance, 20 November 1815, cited in Kertesz (**2**), p. 13.

(**b**) *Metternich was the principal defender of the Vienna Settlement and his anxiety about liberal ideas made him particularly suspicious of the educated classes.*

In all four countries [Germany, Spain, Italy and France] the agitated classes are principally composed of wealthy men – real cosmopolitans, securing their personal advantage at the expense of any order of things whatever – paid State officials, men of letters, lawyers, and the individuals charged with public education.

Metternich's Secret Memorandum to Alexander II in December 1820, at the Congress of Troppau, cited in Bridges *et al.* (**1**), pp. 124–5.

(**c**) *In practical terms Metternich sought to control the activities of the German universities.*

THE UNIVERSITY LAW

1. The duty of this commissioner shall be to watch over the most rigorous observation of the laws and disciplinary regulations; to observe carefully the spirit with which the professors are guided in the scientific courses, or in the method of instruction, to give the instruction a salutary direction, suited to the future destiny of the students, and to devote a constant attention to everything which may tend to the maintenance of morality, good order and decency among the youths . . .
2. The Governments of the States members of the confederation reciprocally engage to remove from their universities . . . the professors and other public teachers against whom it may be proved that in departing from their duty, in overstepping the bounds of their duty, in abusing their legitimate influence over the minds of youth, by the propagation of pernicious dogmas, hostile to order and public tranquillity.

The Carlsbad Decrees, 20 September 1819, cited in Kertesz (**2**), pp. 67–9.

documents 2a–f

New political ideas

(**a**) *Liberalism in the nineteenth century usually demanded a set of freedoms and a broadening of the scope of political participation to include the middle classes.*

1. We demand that our State Governments repudiate the Carlsbad resolutions of 1819 . . . These resolutions violate our inalienable human rights . . .

2. We demand freedom of the press: we must no longer be deprived of the inalienable right of the human spirit to publish its thought without mutilation.
3. We demand freedom of conscience and of learning . . .
4. We demand that the army swear an oath to the constitution.
5. We demand personal freedom. The police must stop its tutelage and torture of the citizen. The right of association, healthy community life . . . the individual's right to move freely in the territory of the German Fatherland . . . must remain undisturbed in future.

The Offenburg Resolutions of the South West German Radicals, 10 September 1847, cited in Kertesz (**2**), pp. 77–9.

Nationalism

(**b**) *Nationalists in the first half of the nineteenth century tended to be liberal in outlook.*

Liberty – Equality – Humanity – Independence – Unity

Section 1
Young Italy is a brotherhood of Italians who believe in a law of Progress and Duty, and are convinced that Italy is destined to become one nation . . . They join this association in the firm intent of consecrating both thought and action to the great aim of reconstituting Italy as one independent sovereign nation of free men and equals.

Section 2
By Italy we understand: 1, Continental and peninsular Italy, bounded on the north by the upper circle of the Alps, on the south by the sea, on the west by the mouths of the Varo, and on the east by Trieste; 2, the islands proved Italian by the language of the inhabitants, and destined, under a special administrative organisation, to form a part of the Italian political unity.

Mazzini's Instructions for the Members of Young Italy, 1831, cited in Kertesz (**2**), p. 173.

(**c**) *The most vigorous national movements of the first half of the nineteenth century developed in Germany and Italy. Both Germans and Italians could call* *upon a 'great Past'. The nationalities of the Habsburg Empire found this more difficult. The timidity of the Czech national movement may be explained by the lack of a 'great Past'.*

I am a Czech of Slavonic blood, and with all the little I possess and all the little I can do, I have devoted myself for all time to the service of my nation. The nation is a small one, it is true, but from time immemorial it has been a nation of itself and based upon its own strength. Its rulers were from olden times members of the federation of German Princes, but the nation never regarded itself as pertaining to the German nation, nor throughout all the centuries was it regarded by others as so pertaining. The whole union of the Czech lands, first with the Holy Roman (German) Empire and then with the German Confederation, was always a mere dynastic tie of which the Czech nation, the Czech estates, scarcely desired to know anything and to which they paid no regard . . . The whole world is well aware that the German Emperors had never, in virtue of their imperial dignity, the slightest to do with the Czech nation; that they possessed neither legislative, nor judicial, nor executive power either in Bohemia or over the Czechs; that they never had the right to raise troops or any royalties from that country; that Bohemia together with its crown lands was never considered as pertaining to any of the one-time ten German States; that appurtenance to the Reich Supreme Court of Justice never applied to it, and so on . . .

The second reason which prevents me from taking part in your deliberations is the fact that, according to all I have so far learned of your aims and intentions as publicly proclaimed, it is your irrevocable desire and purpose to undermine Austria as an independent empire and indeed to make her impossible for all time to come – an empire whose preservation, integrity and consolidation is, and must be, a great important matter not only for my own nation but also for the whole of Europe . . .

You know, gentlemen, what Power it is that holds the entire east of our Continent. You know that this Power, now grown to vast dimensions, increases and expands of itself decade by decade in far greater measure than is possible for the countries of the West. You know that, secure at its own centre against practically every attack, it has become, and has for a long time been, a menace to its neighbours; and that, although it has unhindered access to the North, it is nevertheless, led by natural instinct, always seeking, and will continue to seek, to extend its borders southwards.

Frantisek Palacky's Letter to the Committee of Fifty of the Frankfurt Parliament, 11 April 1848, cited in Bridges *et al.* (**1**), pp. 136–7.

(**d**) *Magyar nationalism, although apparently liberal, also had ambitions to dominate the minorities of the eastern part of the Habsburg Empire.*

DEMANDS OF THE HUNGARIAN PEOPLE
1 Freedom of the press; abolition of censorship.
2 A responsible ministry with its seat in the capital.
3 An annual parliament in Budapest.
4 Political and religious equality before the law.
5 A national guard.
6 Taxes to be paid by all.
7 Abolition of serfdom.
8 Jury system. Equality of representation.
9 A national bank.
10 The military to take an oath to the constitution; Hungarian soldiers not to be stationed abroad, foreign soldiers to be removed.
11 Political prisoners to be freed.
12 Union with Transylvania.

[*The speaking of Magyar was to be a qualification for all members of the parliament.*]

Demands of the Hungarian People, 15 March 1848, cited in Kertesz (**2**), pp. 125–6.

Socialism–communism

(**e**) *The variety of opinions subsumed under the heading 'socialism-communism' is enormous. In the nineteenth century both socialists and communists believed that the democratic principles which had inspired the French Republic of 1792 would never be achieved unless the economic base of society was changed.*

COMMUNIST MANIFESTO
1 Abolition of property in land and application of all rents of land to public purposes.
2 A heavy progressive or graduated income tax.
3 Abolition of all right of inheritance.
4 Confiscation of the property of all emigrants and rebels.

5 Centralisation of credit in the hands of the State, by means of a national bank with State capital and an exclusive monopoly.

6 Centralisation of the means of communication and transport in the hands of the State.

7 Extension of factories and instruments of production owned by the State; the bringing into cultivation of waste-lands, and the improvement of the soil generally in accordance with a common plan.

8 Equal obligation of all to work. Establishment of industrial armies, especially for agriculture.

9 Combination of agriculture with manufacturing industries; gradual abolition of the distinction between town and country, by a more equable distribution of the population over the country.

10 Free education for all children in public schools. Abolition of children's factory labour in its present form. Combination of education with industrial production.

Manifesto of the Communist Party, January 1848, cited in Marx and Engels (**3**), pp. 52–3.

(**f**) *It would seem that Marx and Engels used the word 'communist' in the Manifesto of 1848 for polemical reasons and to distinguish their revolutionary position from that of other Utopian thinkers.*

Nevertheless, when it appeared we could not have called it a *socialist manifesto*. In 1847 two kinds of people were considered socialists. On the one hand were the adherents of the various utopian systems, notably the Owenites in England and the Fourierists in France, both of whom at that date had already dwindled to mere sects gradually dying out. On the other, the manifold types of social quacks who wanted to eliminate social abuses through their various universal panaceas and all kinds of patchwork, without hurting capital and profit in the least. In both cases, people who stood outside the labour movement and who looked for support rather to the 'educated' classes. The section of the working class, however, which demanded a radical reconstruction of society, convinced that mere political revolutions were not enough, then called itself *Communist*. It was still a rough-hewn, only instinctive, and frequently crude communism.

Engels' Preface to the German edition of 1890, cited in Marx and Engels (**3**), pp. 33–4.

The condition of the workers in the years of crisis

The 1830s and 1840s were years of acute social distress. Middle-class observers became increasingly concerned about the condition of the poor.

(**a**) *Living conditions of workers in Lille*

A succession of islets separated by dark narrow alleyways; at the other end are small yards called *courettes* which serve as sewers and rubbish-dumps. In every season of the year there is damp. The apartment windows and the cellar doors all open onto the disease-ridden alleyways, and in the background there are pieces of iron railing over cess-pits which are used day and night as public lavatories. The dwellings are ranged round these plague-spots . . . The further the visitor penetrates these little yards, the more he is surrounded by a strange throng of anaemic, hunchbacked and deformed children with deathly pale livid faces, begging for alms. Most of these wretches are almost naked and even the best-cared-for have rags sticking to them. But these creatures at least breathe fresh air; only in the depths of the cellars can one appreciate the agonies of those who cannot be allowed out on account of their age or the cold weather. For the most part they lie on bare soil, on wisps of rape-straw, on a rough couch of dried potato peelings, on sand or on shavings which have been painstakingly collected during the day's work. The pit in which they languish is bare of any fittings; only those who are best-off possess a temperamental stove, a wooden chair and some cooking utensils. 'I may not be rich,' an old woman told us, pointing to her neighbour lying full-length on the damp cellar floor, 'but I still have my bundle of straw, thank God!' More than three thousand of our fellow-citizens lead this horrifying existence in the Lille cellars.

Adolphe Blanqui, *Les Classes Ouvrieres en France pendant l'Année 1848*, Paris, 1849, cited in Kuczynski (**28**), pp. 93–4.

(**b**) *It is worth considering whether a distinct proletarian culture and consciousness was emerging in the years before 1848. The development of a special 'revolutionary consciousness' has a special place for the historians of the left* (**20, 24, 28, 46**).

. . . the proletarian is aware of his situation. This is why he is fundamentally different from the pauper, who accepts his fate as a divine ordinance and demands nothing but alms and an idle life. The proletarian realised straight away that he was in a situation which was intolerable and unjust . . . moreover he was aware of his strength . . . he saw how the world trembled before him and this recollection emboldened him; he went so far as to disregard Law and Justice. Hitherto property had been a right: he branded it as robbery.

Anon., written in Magdeburg, 1884, cited in Kuczynski (**28**), p. 81.

documents 4a–c
Bread

There is little doubt that the poorest sections of the population spent a large proportion of their incomes on starch foods. Any fluctuation in the prices of these staple foods would have serious repercussions.

(**a**) STANDARD OF LIVING DATA (PRICES)

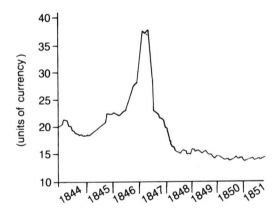

E. Labrousse (**73**).

(**b**) *The agricultural crisis in France originated with the potato blight. At the same time the grain harvests of 1845 and 1846, particularly in the area of the Paris basin, were especially poor, causing prices to soar. Ironically, prices were falling by the autumn of 1847. The relationship between the food crisis and the revolutions is not clear-cut.*

STANDARD OF LIVING DATA (PRICES)

Hamburg

(1841 = 100)

	Wheat	Rye	Barley	Oats
1841	100.0	100.0	100.0	100.0
1842	136.4	83.3	98.7	86.4
1843	103.1	83.3	105.2	94.9
1844	109.4	72.7	105.2	101.7
1845	89.5	59.5	113.0	91.5
1846	129.6	91.7	115.6	111.9
1847	151.8	120.8	185.7	149.1
1848	134.0	82.7	124.7	110.2
1849	100.0	53.5	103.9	69.5
1850	100.0	53.5	93.5	72.9

Konigsberg

(1841–2 = 100)

	Wheat	Rye
1841–42	100.0	100.0
1843–44	70.9	82.7
1845–46	96.5	131.7
1847–48	108.1	128.8
1849–50	80.8	69.2

Berne

(1846 = 100)

	Bread	Potatoes
1836	85.0	
1845	85.0	
1846	100.0	100.0
1847	140.0	136.4
1848	80.0	74.5
1849	75.0	60.9
1850	80.0	65.5

Statistics based on Mulhall (**5**).

Venice

	Wheat	*Maize*
1845	100	
1846	114.4	
1847	196.8	
1845		100
1846		163.6
1847		177.3

Statistics based on P. Ginsborg (**174**).

(c) *Whatever the precise relationship between food prices and the generation of unrest, it is clear that when unrest did break out it was a shocking experience for the respectable classes.*

The cities were full of poor begging for bread, and were invaded by great hordes of peasants, human carcasses with sunken eyes, who could hardly stagger along with the aid of a stick, and who pleaded for something to eat with faint voices and deadened gaze ... The countryside did not present a less terrible or mournful experience. The destitute wandered from villa to villa begging for sustenance ... they eagerly devoured the ears of corn which were not yet ripe ...

Memoirs of Guiseppe Olivi, President of the Department of Treviso in Habsburg Venetia, cited in Ginsborg (**174**).

document 5

The influence of the clergy

*The elections for the Constituent Assembly in France in April 1848 were the subject of a great conflict between the republicans and the clergy. The bishops took direct action in trying to influence the election results (**80**, **86**).*

INSTRUCTIONS TO PARISH PRIESTS

We remind you of your obligation ... to urge upon your parishioners the need to fulfil loyally their sacred duty as voters.

We know, dear colleague, the proper confidence they have in you. So help them with your good advice at this important juncture. Teach them how they should both select their candidate and exercise voting rights. Overcome their objections. Sweep away their fears.

Take pains to explain to them that they are faced with the need to reconcile major interests and must banish all idea of party prejudice. They must concern themselves with one thing only, namely with choosing as their representatives men of recognised integrity who are frankly resolved to set up a Republic in France that respects the sacred rights of religion, liberty, property and the family . . .

Finally, dearly beloved colleague, set your parishioners a good example. Go to the polls at the head of your congregation.

Instructions from the Bishop of Rennes to his clergy, cited in Price (**6**), p. 92.

The prelude to June

documents 6a–b

(**a**) *Alexis de Tocqueville anticipated the events of June 1848.*

In that city there were a hundred thousand armed workmen formed into regiments, without work and dying of hunger. Society was cut in two: those who had nothing united in common envy; those who had anything united in common terror. There were no longer ties of sympathy linking these two great classes, and a struggle was everywhere assumed to be inevitable soon . . .

Alexis de Tocqueville, *Recollections*, cited in Price (**6**), pp. 96–7.

(**b**)
I have carefully noted the nature of these gatherings seen in the street over the last fortnight, of the speeches made by the ringleaders, and the fact that the manufacturers can neither get the workers back into their workshops, where there is employment for them, nor even keep those who had remained. This has led me to the conviction that a hostile organisation is behind these disorders. The alliance is organised by the delegates to the Luxembourg.

Report of the Paris Prefect of Police, 3 June 1848, cited in Price (**6**), p. 100.

June

(a) *Marx saw the June Days uprising as the climax of a class conflict.*

The Paris workers have been overwhelmed by superior forces; they have not succumbed to them. They have been beaten, but it is their enemies who have been vanquished. The momentary triumph of brutal violence has been purchased with the destruction of all the deceptions and illusions of the February revolution, with the dissolution of the whole of the old republican party, and with the fracturing of the French nation into two nations, the nation of the possessors and the nation of the workers. The tricolour republic now bears only one colour, the colour of the defeated, the colour of blood. It has become the red republic.

K. Marx, *Neue Rheinische Zeitung*, cited in Fernbach (**4**), pp. 129–30.

(b) *De Tocqueville considered that the June Days was a manifestation of class conflict, but he did not regard it as a legitimate conflict.*

In truth it was not a political struggle . . . but a class struggle, a sort of 'Servile War'. It stood in the same relation to the facts of the February Revolution as the theory of socialism stood to its ideas; or rather it sprang naturally from those ideas, as a son from his mother; and one should not see it only as brutal and blind, but as a powerful effort of the workers to escape from the necessities of their condition, which had been depicted to them as an illegitimate depression, and by the sword to open up a road towards that imaginary well-being that had been shown to them in the distance as a right. It was this mixture of greedy desires and false theories that engendered the insurrection and made it so formidable. These poor people had been assured that the goods of the wealthy were in some way the result of a theft committed against themselves. They had been assured that inequalities of fortune were as much opposed to morality and the interests of society as to nature. This obscure and mistaken conception of right, combined with brute force, imparted to it an energy, tenacity and strength it would never have had on its own.

Alexis de Tocqueville (**7**), pp. 169–70.

Documents

(c) *The nature of the June conflict is still a source of debate among modern historians. An examination of the occupations of the insurrectionaries has been of special interest.*

CHARACTERISTICS, BY INDUSTRY, OF THOSE ARRESTED FOR PARTICIPATING IN THE JUNE DAYS

Occupational categories	Number of individuals	Percentage of total	Percentage of working population	Percentage married	Median age
Textiles	344	3.1	4.9	75.0	36
Clothing	1044	9.3	17.2	56.5	33
Luxury trades	212	1.9	3.5	84.2	32
Printing and paper	444	3.9	3.0	55.6	31
Metal trades	1325	11.8	2.9	57.3	31
Precious metal trades	239	2.1	1.9	72.7	29
Food	463	4.1	6.7	51.3	32
Furnishing and timber	678	6.0	4.0	62.7	31
Leather	168	1.5	0.6	56.8	32
Coach building	195	1.7	1.0	58.0	32
Chemicals	148	1.3	0.9	54.5	34
Coopers and basketmakers	136	1.2	1.2	67.6	31
Building	2075	18.4	6.6	58.7	32
Transport	529	4.7	2.1	58.2	34
Retail trades	789	7.0	4.7	67.8	34
Liberal and financial professions and students	326	2.9	13.6	57.3	34
Soldiers	501	4.4	4.5	60.3	31
Service and other workers	1640	14.6	20.6	57.6	35
Unknown	456	–	–	66.7	33
TOTAL	11,722	99.9	99.9	59.6	33

L. H. Lees and C. Tilly in (**80**).

Chronology of Events

1848

January	12	Revolution in Palermo, Sicily
February	24	Abdication of Louis Philippe
	25	First Proclamation of the Provisional Government in France
	26	Proclamation of the French Second Republic
	27	Establishment of National Workshops
March	5	Meeting of Heidelberg Liberals calls for a *Vorparlament*
	7	Lamartine's Manifesto to Europe
	13	Resignation of Metternich
	14–15	Formulation of the Demands of the Hungarians
	15	Violence breaks out in Berlin
	18	Frederick William IV promises reform
	23	Piedmont declares war against the Habsburgs
April	10	Prussian troops enter Schleswig-Holstein
	23	Election of the Constituent Assembly in France
May	17	Habsburg Imperial Court leaves Vienna for Innsbruck
	18	Meeting of the Frankfurt *Parlament*
June	2	Meeting of the Pan-Slav Congress in Prague
	16	Windischgratz bombards Prague
	23–26	'June Days' uprising in Paris
July	22	Constituent Assembly meets in Vienna
	23	Radetzky defeats Italians at Custozza
August	26	Prussia accepts the armistice of Malmo, bringing the war over Schleswig-Holstein to an end
September	11	Jellacic begins invasion of Hungary

October	6	'October Days' uprising in Vienna
	31	Military occupation of Vienna by Windischgratz
November	21	Schwarzenberg becomes Habsburg Chancellor
	24	The Pope leaves Rome
December	2	Emperor Ferdinand abdicates in favour of Franz-Josef
	10	Louis Napoléon elected President of Second Republic in France

1849

February	9	Establishment of Roman Republic by Mazzini
March	7	Schwarzenberg dissolves Austrian Constituent Assembly
	23	Final defeat of Italians at Novarra
April	3	Frederick William IV rejects Frankfurt Assembly's offer of the crown of a united Germany
June	13	Demonstrations in Paris protesting at French suppression of the Roman Republic
July	3	French troops occupy Rome
August	13	Hungarians surrender

1850

May	26	Prussia establishes Erfurt Union
November	29	Prussia forced to accept the re-establishment of the German *Diet* by the agreement of Olmutz

1851

December	2	Louis Napoléon's *coup d'état* overthrows the French Second Republic

Glossary

Massimo d'Azeglio   Moderate liberal politician from Piedmont who supported the idea that Italy should be united as a constitutional monarchy ruled by the King of Piedmont-Sardinia.

Alexander Bach   Austrian lawyer who was a leading member of the liberal reform movement in Vienna before 1848. After the revolution he became a member of Schwarzenberg's government, becoming increasingly conservative in his views.

Louis Blanc   French socialist who supported the Banquet campaign. From February to May 1848 he presided over the Luxembourg Commission which was responsible for labour affairs and the administration of the National Workshops. Following the June uprising he fled to England.

Auguste Blanqui   French socialist revolutionary and professional conspirator. He organised many secret revolutionary societies and attempted an armed uprising in 1839.

Stephan Born   German socialist and labour leader who organised a workers' committee in Berlin, which later led to the holding of an all-German workers' congress in August 1848, which subsequently set up a German workers' association, but its membership never exceeded 12,000.

Dynastic Opposition   Section of the French Chamber of Deputies led by Odilon Barrot who opposed Guizot in the 1840s and advocated electoral reform. Many members of the Dynastic Opposition were active in the Banquet campaign.

Ludwig Ficquelmont   Conservative Austrian aristocrat who had served the Habsburgs before 1848 and who was appointed Foreign Minister after the fall of Metternich. He was forced to resign following student demonstrations in May 1848.

Vincenzo Gioberti   Leading thinker-politician of the Italian *Risorgimento* who believed that Italy should be united into a federation under the presidency of the Pope, but with the military protection of Piedmont.

Francesco Guerazzi   Active republican-democrat in Tuscany who became Minister of the Interior in a short-lived republican government in Tuscany in 1848.

François Guizot   French conservative politician who was Louis Philippe's Prime Minister, 1840–48. His stubborn opposition to demands for electoral reform was a significant cause of the February revolution in France.

Industrial Code   Set of demands put forward by German workers in 1848, including the preservation of worker guilds.

Francis Kolowrat   Austrian aristocrat and rival to Metternich between 1835 and 1848. His manoeuvrings in the Habsburg Court did much to render Metternich ineffective in his last years in office and contributed ultimately to the latter's downfall.

Kossuth's speech at Pressburg   Delivered at the Hungarian *Diet* in March 1848, it attacked the Habsburg monarchy and outlined the case for Hungarian independence. Its subsequent translation into German and publication in Vienna reinforced the liberal constitutional movement in the Empire.

Luddism   Early form of labour protest which involved workers smashing machines which had made them unemployed.

Daniele Manin   Venetian lawyer and republican politician who became President of the short-lived Venetian Republic, 1848–49.

Giuseppe Mazzini   Italian republican nationalist. He was the most important figure before 1848 for articulating republican-national feeling. He was involved in many plots and unsuccessful uprisings before 1848 and established the Young Italy movement in 1831. He was briefly President of the Roman Republic in March 1849.

Louis-Mathieu Molé   French politician of conservative-moderate views who had been Louis Philippe's Foreign Minister in the early 1830s. He found himself in opposition during the 1840s and was a bitter opponent of Guizot. In February 1848 Louis Philippe dismissed the latter in favour of Molé in a vain attempt to stem the revolutionary tide.

Montagnards   Term used in 1792–93 to identify those deputies, led by Robespierre, Danton and Marat, who had instigated the formation of the republic. By the mid-nineteenth century the term was generally associated with the extreme left of the republican tradition.

National Workshops Scheme　Series of public works set up by the provisional government in France in an attempt to solve the problem of unemployment. The programme was abolished in June 1848 and contributed to the uprising of that month.

Quadrilateral　Group of four fortresses in northern Italy – Verona, Peschiera, Mantua and Legnano – used by the Austrian armies in the war against the Italians, 1848–49.

Josef Radetzky　Experienced Austrian soldier who had fought against Napoleon. He became commander-in-chief of the Austrian garrison in Lombardy in 1831. He defeated the Piedmontese armies at Custozza in July 1848 and at Novarra in March 1849.

Josef von Radowitz　Prussian aristocrat and supporter of King Frederick William IV. Although he was a conservative he recognised the need to follow enlightened social policies. He became Foreign Minister of Prussia in 1849.

Robot　Form of feudal labour service performed by peasants in large parts of the Habsburg Empire. Peasants were expected to perform labour service for their landlords for so many days in the year as a kind of rent. It was a source of considerable resentment among the peasants and its abolition in 1848–49 was both a major achievement and a significant cause of the peasants subsequently losing interest in the revolution.

Henri Saint-Simon　French economic thinker who believed that the state could plan and organise economic activity. His ideas influenced socialists like Louis Blanc, as well as Louis Napoléon, later Emperor of France, who used the power of the state to promote the growth of the French economy.

Archduchess Sophie　Wife of Archduke Charles who was the brother of Ferdinand, Emperor, 1835–48. Sophie was the mother of Franz-Josef who became Emperor in 1848, following the abdication of Ferdinand. She attracted support from those in the Court who opposed Metternich in the years immediately before 1848, including Kolowrat. She was a determined woman who became the focal point of counter-revolutionary interest in 1848–49.

Francis Stadion　Austrian civil servant who became Minister of the

Interior in Schwarzenberg's government in November 1848. He was largely responsible for drafting the new constitution after 1848 and laying the foundations for a more effective administration of the Empire.

Stephen Szechenyi   Hungarian economic thinker who attacked Habsburg feudalism. His ideas on agricultural improvement and economic liberalism generally did much to fuel Hungarian nationalism. He was briefly a member of Kossuth's independent Hungarian government.

Alexis de Tocqueville   Liberal-minded French aristocrat who had written extensively on the history of France. He was a deputy in the French Chamber from 1839 to 1848. He was elected to the Constituent Assembly in 1848 and helped draft the constitution of the new republic. He was briefly Foreign Minister of the Second Republic during 1849 but resigned in protest at the growing authoritarianism of Louis Napoléon.

Wenzelsbad Meeting   Held on 11 March 1848 in the Wenzelsbad inn, a hostelry frequented by liberal and nationalist politicians in Prague. On this occasion a twelve-point programme was drawn up containing the familiar liberal demands – freedom of the press, abolition of the *Robot*, etc.

Bibliography

PRIMARY SOURCES

1 Bridges, R. C., Dukes, P., Hargreaves, J. D. and Scott, W. (eds), *Nations and Empires: Documents on the History of Europe and on its Relations with the World* (Macmillan, 1969).

2 Kertesz, G. A. (ed.), *Documents in the Political History of the European Continent 1815–1939* (Oxford University Press, 1968).

3 Marx, K. and Engels, F., *Selected Works*, particularly 'The Eighteenth Brumaire of Louis Bonaparte' and 'Class Struggles in France 1848 to 1850' (Lawrence and Wishart, 1968).

4 Marx, K. and Engels, F., *The Revolutions of 1848*, ed. D. Fernbach (Penguin, 1973).

5 Mulhall, M., *A Dictionary of Statistics* London (1892).

6 Price, R. (ed.), *1848 in France* (Thames and Hudson, 1975).

7 De Tocqueville, A., *Recollections*, ed. J. P. Mayer and A. P. Kerr (Macdonald, 1970).

GENERAL BOOKS

8 Abendroth, W., *A Short History of the European Working Class* (New Left Books, 1972).

9 Anderson, M. S., *The Ascendancy of Europe: Aspects of European History 1815–1914* (Longman, 1972).

10 Artz, F. B., *Reaction and Revolution 1814–1832* (Harper and Row, 1977).

11 Bury, J. P. T., *The New Cambridge Modern History*, Vol. X: *The Zenith of European Power: 1830–1870* (Cambridge University Press, 1960).

12 Carr, E. H., *Studies in Revolution* (Macmillan, 1950).

13 Caute, D., *The Left in Europe* (Weidenfeld and Nicolson, 1966).

14 Cipolla, C. M. (ed.), *The Fontana Economic History of Europe*, Vols III and IV (Fontana-Collins, 1973).

15 Collins, I., *The Age of Progress* (Edward Arnold, 1964).

16 Crawley, C. E., *The New Cambridge Modern History*, Vol. IX: *War and Peace in an Age of Upheaval* (Cambridge University Press, 1965).

17 Droz, J., *Europe Between Revolutions* (Fontana-Collins, 1967).

127

Bibliography

18 Fasel, G., *Europe in Upheaval: The Revolutions of 1848* (Rand McNally, 1970).

19 Fetjo, F., *The Opening of an Era: 1848, an Historical Symposium* (Allan Wingate, 1948).

20 Foster, J., *Class Struggle and the Industrial Revolution* (Weidenfeld and Nicolson, 1974).

21 Geary, D., *European Labour Protest 1848–1939* (Croom Helm, 1981).

22 Grenville, J. A. S., *Europe Reshaped 1848–1878* (Fontana-Collins, 1976).

23 Hobsbawm, E. J., *The Age of Capital: Europe from 1848 to 1875* (Weidenfeld and Nicolson, 1974).

24 Hobsbawm, E. J., *The Age of Revolution: Europe 1789–1848* (Weidenfeld and Nicolson, 1962).

25 Kamenka, E. and Smith, F. B., *Intellectuals and the Revolution: Socialism and the Experience of 1848* (Edward Arnold, 1979).

26 Kranzberg, M., *1848: A Turning Point?* (D.C. Heath, 1959).

27 Kuczynski, J., *Labour Conditions in Western Europe 1820 to 1935* (Lawrence and Wishart, 1937).

28 Kuczynski, J., *The Rise of the Working Class* (Weidenfeld and Nicolson, 1967).

29 Kuczynski, J., *A Short History of Labour Conditions in Germany 1800 to the Present Day* (Lawrence and Wishart, 1945).

30 Langer, W. L., *Political and Social Upheaval 1832–1852* (Harper and Row, 1969).

31 Leslie, R. F., *The Age of Transformation 1789–1871* (Blandford, 1964).

32 Lichtheim, G., *A Short History of Socialism* (Weidenfeld and Nicolson, 1970).

33 Merriman, J. (ed.), *Consciousness and Class Experience* (Holmes and Meier, 1979).

34 Minogue, K., *Nationalism* (Batsford, 1967).

35 Moraze, C., *The Triumph of the Middle Classes: A Study in European Values in the Nineteenth Century* (Weidenfeld and Nicolson, 1966).

36 McLellan, D., *Karl Marx: His Life and Thought* (Macmillan, 1973).

37 Namier, L., *The Revolution of the Intellectuals* (Hamish Hamilton, 1946).

38 Price, R., *The Revolutions of 1848* (Macmillan, 1988).

39 Robertson, P., *Revolutions of 1848: A Social History* (Princeton University Press, 1952).

40 Rudé, G., *The Crowd in History* (Wiley, 1966).

41 Stearns, P., *European Society in Upheaval: A Social History since 1800* (Macmillan, 1967).

42 Stearns, P., *The 1848 Revolutions* (Weidenfeld and Nicolson, 1974).

43 Taylor, A. J. P., *Europe: Grandeur and Decline* (Penguin, 1967).

44 Taylor, A. J. P., *The Struggle for Mastery in Europe 1848–1918* (Oxford University Press, 1954).

45 Thomson, D., *Europe Since Napoleon* (Longman, 1962).

46 Thompson, E. P., *The Making of the English Working Class* (Gollancz, 1968).

47 Woodward, E. L., *Three Studies in European Conservatism: Metternich, Guizot and the Catholic Church in the Nineteenth Century* (Constable, 1929).

48 Wrigley, E. A., *Population and History* (Weidenfeld and Nicolson, 1966).

GENERAL ARTICLES

49 Amman, P., 'The changing outlines of 1848', *American Historical Review*, lxviii, no. 4 (1962), 938–58.

50 Amman, P., 'Revolution: a redefinition', *Political Science Quarterly*, lxxvii (1962), 36–52.

51 Bergman, M., 'The potato blight in the Netherlands', *International Review of Social History*, xii (1967), 390–431.

52 Briggs, A., 'The language of class in the nineteenth century', in A. Briggs and J. Saville (eds), *Essays in Labour History* (Macmillan, 1967).

53 Gillis, J. R., 'Political decay and the European revolutions 1789–1848', *World Politics*, xii (1970), 344–90.

54 Harris, D., 'European liberalism in the nineteenth century', *American Historical Review*, lx, no. 3 (1955), 501–26.

55 Labrousse, E., '1848–1830–1789: How revolutions are born', in Crouzet, F., Chaloner, W. H. and Stern, W. M. (eds), *Essays in European Economic History* (Edward Arnold, 1969).

56 O'Boyle, L., 'The middle classes in western Europe, 1815–1848', *American Historical Review*, lxx, no. 3 (1966), 126–45.

57 O'Boyle, L., 'The problem of an excess of educated men in western Europe 1800–1850', *Journal of Modern History*, xlii, no. 4 (1970), 471–95.

58 Stedman Jones, G., 'The mid-century crisis and the 1848 revolutions', *Theory and Society*, xii (1983).

59 Tilly, C., 'The changing place of collective violence', in

Richter, M. (ed.), *Essays in Theory and History* (Harvard University Press, 1970).

FRANCE

Books

60 Agulhon, M., *The Republican Experiment 1848–52* (Cambridge University Press, 1983).

61 Agulhon, M., *The Republic in the Village: The People of the Var from the French Revolution to the Second Republic* (Cambridge University Press, 1982).

62 Aminzade, R., *Class Politics and Early Industrial Capitalism* (University of New York Press, 1981).

63 Bury, J. P. T., *France 1814–1940* (Methuen, 1962).

64 Chevalier, L., *Labouring Classes and Dangerous Classes in Paris During the First Half of the Nineteenth Century* (Routledge, 1973).

65 Cobban, A., *A History of Modern France*, Vol. II (Penguin, 1961).

66 Collingham, H. A. C., *The July Monarchy: A Political History of France 1830–48* (Longman, 1988).

67 Denholm, A., *France in Revolution: 1848* (Wiley, 1972).

68 Duveau, G., *1848: The Making of a Revolution* (Routledge, 1967).

69 Gossez, R., *Les Ouvriers de Paris* (Paris, 1967).

70 Howarth, T. E. B., *Citizen King: The Life of Louis Philippe, King of the French* (Eyre and Spottiswoode, 1961).

71 Jardin, A. and Tudesq, A. J., *Restoration and Reaction 1815–48* (Cambridge University Press, 1983).

72 Johnson, D., *Guizot: Aspects of French History 1787–1874* (Routledge, 1963).

73 Labrousse, E. (ed.), *Aspects de la crise et de la dépression de l'économie française au milieu du XIXe siècle, 1846–52* (Société d'Histoire de la Révolution, 1956).

74 Lamartine, A., *History of the French Revolution of 1848* (London, 1857).

75 Magraw, R., *France 1815–1914: The Bourgeois Century* (Fontana, 1983).

76 Merriman, J. M., *The Agony of the Republic: The Repression of the Left in Revolutionary France 1848–51* (Yale University Press, 1978).

77 Palmade, G., *French Capitalism in the Nineteenth Century* (David and Charles, 1972).

78 Price, R., *An Economic History of Modern France 1730–1914* (Macmillan, 1981).

79 Price, R., *The French Second Republic: A Social History* (Batsford, 1972).

80 Price, R. (ed.), *Revolution and Reaction*; see especially L. H. Lees and C. Tilly, 'The People of June' (Croom Helm, 1975).

81 Sewell, W. H., *Work and Revolution in France: The Language of Labour from the Old Regime to 1848* (Cambridge University Press, 1980).

82 Stearns, P., *Paths to Authority: The Middle Class and the Industrial Labour Force in France 1820–48* (University of Illinois, 1978).

83 Zeldin, T., *France 1848–1945: Politics and Anger* (Oxford University Press, 1979).

84 Zeldin, T., *The Political System of Napoleon III* (Macmillan, 1958).

Articles

85 Amman, P., 'A Journée in the making: May 15, 1848', *Journal of Modern History*, xlii, no. 1 (1970), 42–69.

86 Amman, P., 'Prelude to insurrection: the Banquet of the People', *French Historical Studies*, i, no. 4 (1960), 436–40.

87 Amman, P., 'Recent Writings on the French Second Republic', *Journal of Modern History*, xxxiv, no. 4 (1962), 409–29.

88 Baughman, J. J., 'The French Banquet Campaign of 1847–48', *Journal of Modern History*, xxxi (1959), 1–15.

89 Bezucha, R. J., 'The "preindustrial" worker movement: the canuts of Lyons', in R. J. Bezucha (ed.), *Modern European Social History* (D. C. Heath, 1972), 93–123.

90 Cobban, A., 'Administrative pressure in the election of the French Constituent Assembly, April 1848', *Bulletin of the Institute of Historical Research* (1952), 133–59.

91 Cobban, A., 'The influence of the clergy and the "Instituteurs Primaires" in the election of the Constituent Assembly, April 1848', *English Historical Review*, lvii (1942), 334–44.

92 Cobban, A., 'The middle classes in France 1815–48', *French Historical Studies*, v, no. 1 (1967), 41–52.

93 Crouzet, F., 'French economic growth in the nineteenth century reconsidered', *History*, lix, no. 196 (1974), 167–79.

94 Dunham, A. L., 'Unrest in France', *Journal of Economic History*, supplement viii (1948), 74–84.

131

95 Fasel, G., 'The French election of April 23, 1848: suggestions for a revision', *French Historical Studies*, v (1968), 285–98.

96 Fasel, G., 'The wrong revolution', *French Historical Studies*, viii, no. 4 (1974).

97 Gossez, R., 'Diversité des antagonismes sociaux vers le milieu du XIXe siècle', *Revue économique*, no. 7 (1956), 439–58.

98 Higgonet, P. and Higgonet, T., 'Class, corruption and politics in the French Chamber of Deputies 1846–48', *French Historical Studies*, v (1967), 204–24.

99 Koepke, R. L., 'The failure of parliamentary government in France 1840–48', *European Studies Review*, ix (1979).

100 Liebman, R., 'Repressive strategies and the working class protest: Lyons 1848–52', *Social Science History*, xi (1980).

101 Loubère, L. A., 'The emergence of the extreme left in the Lower Languedoc, 1848–51: social and economic factors in politics', *American Historical Review*, lxxiii, no. 4 (1968), 1019–51.

102 McPhee, P., 'The seed time of the Republic: society and politics in the Pyrenées-Orientales, 1848–51', *Australian Journal of Political History*, xxii, no. 2 (1970), 195–213.

103 Merriman, J. M., 'Social conflict in France: the Limoges Revolution of April 27, 1848', *Societas*, iv, no. 1 (1974), 21–38.

104 Pinkney, D. H., 'The myth of the Revolution of 1830', in T. Ropp (ed.), *Festschrift for F. B. Artz* (Duke University Press, 1964).

105 Pinkney, D. H., 'A new look at the French Revolution of 1830', *Review of Politics*, xxiii (1961), 490–506.

106 Price, R., 'Techniques of repression: the control of popular protest in mid-nineteenth century France', *Historical Journal*, xxv (1982).

107 Sewell, W. H., 'Social change and the rise of the working class in Marseille', *Past and Present*, no. 65 (1974), 75–109.

108 Stearns, P., 'Patterns of industrial strike activity during the July Monarchy', *American Historical Review*, lxx, no. 2 (1965), 371–95.

109 Weber, E., 'The Second Republic, politics and the peasant', *French Historical Studies*, xi (1980).

GERMANY
Books
110 Blackbourn, D. and Eley, G., *The Peculiarities of German*

History: Bourgeois Society and Politics in Nineteenth Century Germany (Oxford University Press, 1985).

111 Carr, W., *A History of Germany 1815–1985* (Edward Arnold, 1987).

112 Craig, G., *The Politics of the Prussian Army* (Oxford University Press, 1956).

113 Eyck, F., *The Frankfurt Parliament 1848–49* (Macmillan, 1968).

114 Eyck, F. (ed.) *The Revolutions of 1848–49* (Oliver and Boyd, 1972).

115 Gillis, J. R., *The Prussian Bureaucracy in Crisis 1840–1860* (Stanford University Press, 1971).

116 Hamerow, T., *Restoration, Revolution, Reaction: Economics and Politics in Germany 1815–1871* (Princeton University Press, 1958).

118 Holborn, H., *A History of Modern Germany 1840–1945* (Eyre and Spottiswoode, 1969).

119 Mann, G., *The History of Germany Since 1789* (Chatto and Windus, 1968).

120 Noyes, P., *Organisation and Revolution: Working Class Associations in the German Revolution* (Princeton University Press, 1966).

121 Pinson, K., *Modern Germany: Its History and Civilisation* (Macmillan, 1966).

123 Ramm, A., *Germany 1789–1918* (Methuen, 1967).

124 Reichard, R., *Crippled from Birth: German Social Democracy 1844–1870* (Iowa University Press, 1969).

125 Sheehan, J. J., *German History 1770–1866* (Oxford University Press, 1989).

126 Sheehan, J. J., *German Liberalism in the Nineteenth Century* (Chicago University Press, 1978).

127 Stadelmann, K., *Social and Political History of the German 1848 Revolution* (Ohio University Press, 1978).

128 Taylor, A. J. P., *The Course of German History* (Hamish Hamilton, 1945).

129 Valentin, V., *1848: Chapters of German History* (Allen and Unwin, 1940).

Articles

130 Hahn, E., 'German parliamentary national aims in 1848–49: a legacy re-assessed', *Central European History*, xiii (1980), 287–93.

131 Hamerow, T., 'History and the German Revolution of 1848', *American Historical Review*, lx (1954).

132 Hamerow, T., 'The elections to the Frankfurt Parliament', *Journal of Modern History*, xxxiii, no. 1 (1961), 15–32.

133 Hamerow, T., 'The German artisan movement 1848–49', *Journal of Central European Affairs*, xxi (1961), 135–52.

134 Ludtke, A., 'The role of state violence in the period of transition to industrial capitalism: the example of Prussia 1815–48', *Social History*, iii (1979).

135 Mattheisen, D. J., 'History as current events: recent works on the German revolution of 1848', *American Historical Review*, lxxxiii (1983).

136 Mattheisen, D. J., 'Liberal constitutionalism in the Frankfurt Parliament of 1848: an inquiry based on roll-call analysis', *Central European History* , xii (1979), 124–42.

137 O'Boyle, L., 'The democratic left in Germany, 1848', *Journal of Modern History*, xxxiii, no. 4 (1961), 374–83.

138 Orr, W., 'East Prussia and the Revolution of 1848', *Central European History*, xiii (1980), 303–31.

139 Popiolek, F., '1848 in Silesia', *Journal of Central European Affairs*, xxvi (1948), 374–89.

140 Sheehan, J. J., 'Liberalism and society in Germany 1815–48', *Journal of Modern History*, xlv, no. 4 (1973), 583–604.

141 Shorter, E., 'Middle-class anxiety in the German revolution of 1848', *Journal of Social History* (1969), 189–215.

142 Tilly, R., 'Popular disorders in nineteenth century Germany', *Journal of Social History* (1970), 1–40.

143 Zucker, S., 'German women and the revolution of 1848: Kathinka Zitz-Halein and the Humania Association', *Central European History*, xiii (1980), 237–54.

THE HABSBURG EMPIRE
Books

144 Barany, G., *Stephen Szechenyi and the Awakening of Hungarian Nationalism 1791–1841* (Princeton University Press, 1968).

145 Deak, I., *The Lawful Revolution: Louis Kossuth and the Hungarians 1848–49* (Columbia University Press, 1979).

146 Kann, R. A., *The Multinational Empire: Nationalism and National Reform in the Habsburg Empire 1848–1918*, 2 vols (Columbia University Press, 1950).

147 Kann, R. A., *A History of the Habsburg Empire 1526–1918* (University of California Press, 1974).

148 Macartney, C. A., *The Habsburg Empire 1790–1918*, (Weidenfeld and Nicolson, 1969).

149 Macartney, C. A., *Hungary: A Short History* (Edinburgh University Press, 1962).
150 Palmer, A., *Metternich: Councillor of Europe* (Weidenfeld and Nicolson, 1972).
151 Pech, S. Z., *The Czech Revolution of 1848* (University of North Carolina Press, 1969).
152 Rath, R. J., *The Viennese Revolution of 1848* (University of Texas Press, 1957).
153 Sked, A., *The Survival of the Habsburg Empire: Radetzky, the Imperial Army and the Class War, 1848* (Longman, 1979).
154 Taylor, A. J. P., *The Habsburg Monarchy* (Hamish Hamilton, 1949).
155 Ward, D., *1848: The Fall of Metternich* (Hamish Hamilton, 1970).

Articles
156 Barany, G., 'The Szechenyi problem', *Journal of Central and East European Affairs*, xx, no. 3 (1960), 251–69.
157 Hawgood, J. A., '1848 in central Europe: an essay in historical synchronisation', *Slavonic and East European Studies Review*, xxvi (1948), 314–28.
158 Ivanyi, B. G., 'From feudalism to capitalism: the economic background to Szechenyi's reform in Hungary', *Journal of Central and East European Affairs*, xx, no. 3 (1960), 270–88.
159 Lutz, R. R., 'Fathers and sons in the Vienna revolution of 1848', *Journal of Central European Affairs*, xxii, no. 2 (1962), 161–73.
160 Macurek, J., 'The achievements of the Slavonic Congress', *Slavonic and East European Review*, xxvi (1948), 329–40.
161 Wagner, F. S., 'Szechenyi and the nationality problem in the Habsburg Empire', *Journal of Central European Affairs*, xx, no. 3 (1960), 289–311.
162 Zaceck, J. F., 'Palacky and his history of the Czech nation', *Journal of Central European Affairs*, xxxiii, no. 4 (1964), 412–23.

ITALY
Books
163 Ginsborg, P., *Daniel Manin and the Venetian Revolution* (Cambridge University Press, 1979).
164 Hearder, H., *Italy in the Age of the Risorgimento* (Longman, 1983).

Bibliography

165 Lovett, C., *The Democratic Movement in Italy 1830–76* (Harvard University Press, 1982).
166 Mack Smith, D., *Cavour* (Weidenfeld and Nicolson, 1985).
167 Mack Smith, D., *Italy: A Modern History* (University of Michigan, 1969).
168 Mack Smith, D., *The Making of Italy 1796–1866* (Macmillan, 1988).
169 Mack Smith, D., *Victor Emmanuel, Cavour and the Risorgimento* (Oxford University Press, 1971).
170 Procacci, G., *History of the Italian People* (Weidenfeld and Nicolson, 1970).
171 Whyte, A. J., *The Evolution of Modern Italy* (Oxford University Press, 1944).
172 Woolf, S., *A History of Italy 1700–1860: The Social Constraints of Political Change* (Methuen, 1979).

Articles

173 Demarco, D., 'L'économie italienne du nord et du sud avant l'unité', *Revue d'Histoire Économique et Sociale*, xxxiv (1956), 369–91.
174 Ginsborg, P., 'Peasants and revolutionaries in Venice and the Veneto, 1848', *Historical Journal*, xvii (1974), 503–50.

POLAND
Books

175 Davies, N., *The Heart of Europe: A Short History of Poland* (Oxford University Press, 1984).
176 Leslie, R. F., *Reform and Insurrection in Russian Poland* (University of London Press, 1963).
177 Seton-Watson, H., *The Russian Empire 1801–1917* (Oxford University Press, 1967).

Index